Praise for
Playing with Baby

Laurie Hollman, PhD, knows very well the needs of parents and babies and the intensity of their relationships. She captures the essence of the complex and stimulating playfulness that is essential for a good connection with a very young child.

She restores play to a central position and offers rich examples and guidance on pleasurable communication with an infant—so vital now that neuroscience research in infants has demonstrated that emotional attunement is essential for good development.

This is a brilliant book, exciting and very accessible—a good combination of education, emotional support, and psychoanalytic thinking.

—Christine Anzieu-Premmereur, MD, director of
    Parent-Infant Psychotherapy Training at the Columbia
    Psychoanalytic Center

Laurie Hollman captures the magic of play for both parents and babies during the first year of life.

In this original book, specific month-by-month play suggestions are linked to validating state-of-the-art research. Understanding the science behind parent-baby play enriches parents' experience of the baby's developing brain and the deepening parent-baby relationship.

A baby's contagious joy while playing peek-a-boo, sense of wonder shaking a rattle and making it jingle, and power to knock down a tower of blocks and rebuild it together delight parents and babies and evoke parents' embodied memories. All this and more to be discovered in *Playing with Baby*!

—Ilene S. Lefcourt, author of *Parenting and Childhood Memories: A Psychoanalytic Approach to Reverberating Ghosts and Magic* and faculty at Columbia University Center for Psychoanalytic Training and Research Parent-Infant Program

Dr. Laurie Hollman's high regard for her audience, parents of babies, is demonstrated by how clearly she communicates useful information previously only accessible to developmental psychologists and infancy researchers. She illustrates in her book how helpful it is to parents and caregivers of babies to be informed of all the wonderful information revealed by years of research. It is implied over and over that the emotional and physical wellbeing of infants is enhanced when parents know in a thorough way what is going on developmentally in a growing infant's life, step by step, month by month. Furthermore, she provides all sorts of practical ways to implement and further strengthen baby's development through play and care. I would recommend this book to any young parent embarking on the great adventure of being with baby. With Laurie Hollman's book as a guide, the journey will be that much more fulfilling and secure.

—Andrea Remez, PhD, clinical psychologist and parent-infant therapist; faculty, National Institute of Psychoanalysis, New York

Dr. Hollman has done it again—written an invaluable book for parents and caregivers, this time of babies. How does one have a "play date" with a one-month-old or five-month-old? Here you have it. Dr. Hollman distils decades of research and hands-on experience into month-by-month insights, knowledge, and play time, designed to strengthen your bonds with baby in the first year.

—Marcelle Soviero, director of Marcelle Ink, author of *An Iridescent Life: Essays on Motherhood*, and former editor-in-chief and publisher of *Brain Child Magazine* and *Teen Magazine*

An excellent resource for new parents to create a loving relationship with their baby while examining her charming personality during the first year of life. Dr. Laurie Hollman effectively presents how to intensify your baby's social and cognitive development through knowledge-based play techniques. Common questions such as bonding, emotional response, and communication are addressed, providing peace of mind that what you are doing for your baby bestows long-term benefits. *Playing with Baby* provides a clear message: engaging with your baby may just be your most fulfilling job.

—Lisa Lewis, MD, pediatrician and author of *Feed the Baby Hummus: Pediatrician-Backed Secrets from Cultures Around the World*

Playing with Baby

Published by Familius LLC, www.familius.com
PO Box 1249, Reedley, CA 93654

Familius books are available at special discounts for bulk purchases,
whether for sales promotions or for family or corporate use.
For more information, contact Familius Sales at orders@familius.com.

Library of Congress Control Number: 2021933763

Print ISBN 9781641704663
Ebook ISBN 9781641704878

Printed in the United States of America

Edited by Kaylee Mason, Michele Robbins, and Alison Strobel
Cover and book design by Mara Harris
Illustrations by Mara Harris

10 9 8 7 6 5 4 3 2 1

First Edition

Playing with Baby

Research-Based Play to Bond with Your Baby from Birth to One Year

Laurie Hollman, PhD

FAMILIUS

To Jeff, my husband, with whom I've raised two sons, David and Rich, our enchanting babies who have grown to be fine men.

To David and Claire, who are raising two of our grandchildren, Zander and Eddie, who are growing to be exciting children.

To Rich and Shelley, who are raising our third grandchild, infant Hazel, who is beginning her first year with such a lively spirit and joy.

Acknowledgments

As always in my parenting books, I first thank my husband, Jeff, for his tremendous support for the evolution of this book. He enjoys learning about and playing with babies whom we've loved immensely as we've raised them to become fine adults, our sons, David and Rich.

I am grateful to my older son, David, my first wondrous baby, who has grown up to be an industrious and inventive loving man and father with Claire as a superlative mother of their two sons: Zander, age twelve, and Eddie, age nine. They are writing imaginative stories of their own, so we now support each other as authors.

As David and Claire build their own home from the ground up, their sons learn and experience this unfathomable feat that continually churns up their exciting adventures.

My loving appreciation further extends to my younger son, Rich, my second wondrous baby, a hard-working, ingeniously creative, and loving man who is now also a father with Shelley as an endearing mother of their beautiful ten-month-old baby, Hazel. Their deep empathy and love as they communicate together in multiple ways with their growing infant has continued to enrich my always growing knowledge of infancy.

Rich has written the music and lyrics to innumerable songs during these ten months dedicated to Hazel, that he sings with Shelley bringing delight and joy to their growing baby. This wonderful form of communication is enriching for their baby, of course, as well as inspiring for me as a writer about infancy. Rich and Shelley are finding great happiness as parents enjoying playing with little ten-month-old, adorable Hazel, who just began to walk!

It is with these exceptional children and adults that have inspired me, each in their own ways, to write about how babies play that led to my desire to write this book.

These experiences combine with the inspirations of researchers around the world from whom I have learned, many of whom I had the pleasure of studying with in great depth. I am thankful for their outstanding findings that in turn I hope to give to you, my readers, so you, too, have the pleasure of learning about how you and your babies can play happily together with new insights, empathy, and love.

Working with the Familius team as always is gratifying. Thanks to the publisher, Christopher Robbins, for his accessibility and encouragement as I write for Familius. I have also been fortunate to work with two fine editors. Kaylee Mason meticulously read each word, gave thought to my concepts, and succeeded in her collaborative way to refine this book before she went on maternity leave to eventually give birth to her third wonderful baby. Michelle Robbins continued to read and explore my concepts with me as the book was brought to fruition.

Finally, I cannot conclude without fondly thanking Kate Farrell, the Familius publicist whose innovative and tireless efforts to publicize this book, like the many others that preceded it, gave me such pleasure with her encouragement for my writing as she sent this book out to you.

Other Books by the Author

Unlocking Parental Intelligence: Finding Meaning in Your Child's Behavior, Familius, Sanger, Calif., 2015

The Busy Parent's Guide to Managing Anxiety in Children and Teens: The Parental Intelligence Way, Familius, Sanger, Calif., 2018

The Busy Parent's Guide to Managing Anger in Children and Teens: The Parental Intelligence Way, Familius, Sanger, Calif., 2018

The Busy Parent's Guide to Managing Exhaustion in Children and Teens: The Parental Intelligence Way, Familius, Sanger, Calif., 2020

The Busy Parent's Guide to Managing Technology with Children and Teens, The Parental Intelligence Way, Familius, Sanger, Calif., 2020

Are You Living with a Narcissist? How Narcissistic Men Impact Your Happiness, How to Identify Them, and How to Avoid Raising One, Familius, Sanger, Calif., 2020

Contents

Introduction

Newborns are mysterious and fascinating little beings. As parents, we wonder, "What's going on in that tiny head of yours?" But before we dive into the inner workings of your baby's mind, let's discuss what you can expect in this book—all you can discover about this first year.

In order to know how to play with our babies, we need to understand them. This book will not only discuss playing but also the research behind babies enjoying your play and how you can enhance their senses.

What to Expect in This Book

In this book, I will focus on the infant's experience with play based on observations that have taken place in the past decades by several theorists. We will discuss you and your infant's experiences playing together. You will read about emotional signals coming from your infant's behavior and how best to respond in animated ways (Ammaniti and Trentini 2009). As we wonder together about the mental processes that go on in your infant's mind as she plays, it will become evident when she is stimulated, frustrated, or gratified.

From birth, infants live in a two-person social world—you and your baby. That is, they coordinate their behaviors with those of their primary caretaker, who will play with them from the very start (Peery 1980; Trevarthen 1979, 321–347). You will notice how they are alert from their first moments after birth and have active minds and multiple physical and emotional needs. In this book, we will discuss how parents can encourage their babies to learn during their baby's first twelve months—How? Mostly through play!

Babies are dazzling, brilliant, and smart learners. Through play, you can learn how your baby's mind works, how to relate to her, and how to engage with her.

As you will see, babies are looking to interact and engage from the beginning. Yes! From the absolute beginning! At birth, they can differentiate human faces and voices from other sights and sounds—and they prefer them.

Within a few days, babies recognize familiar faces, voices, and smells and prefer them to unfamiliar ones. So, they choose you over others with their gazes. Remarkably, a baby's line of sight or vision is most clearly focused at the distance of a person holding them. It's as if they are "designed to see the people who love them more clearly than anything else" (Gopnik, Meltzoff, and Kuhl 1999, 29). How wonderful!

Babies love novelty. If they see the same picture over and over, they lose interest. Show them something else, and they perk right up!

Babies recognize noises. As a newborn, if a baby hears a noise, he will look in that direction, suggesting he already expects to see something to which the noise directed him. In other words, babies connect sound and vision. By five months old, their minds are even more complex, discriminating between what sound goes with what object or face. Then by the time they are nine months old, they have discovered that something hasn't disappeared when it's been covered or hidden from view. They discover this through repetition. What a fun year of progression you have ahead of you!

Babies do what they see! They are attuned to people and are active imitators early on. Stick out your tongue at a baby, and she will stick out her tongue at you. Similarly, open your mouth and your infant will open hers. This is at one month old! How fast babies learn from us.

"In order to imitate, newborn babies must somehow understand the similarity between an internal feeling and the external face they see, like a round shape with a long pink thing at the bottom moving back and forth [the tongue]" (30). Further, babies seem to know things have three dimensions. They know that something that *looks* curved also *feels* curved (63)!

From the time they are born they seem to be in touch with their movements, aches, and tickles. This is a very early recognition of their personal self. From birth, they also sense somehow that their bodily movements of that growing personal self are like yours. So, they notice movements of yours they can see yet not feel (30).

While we know that babies love human voices and faces, they also show interest in stripes and edges. You can show your babies different pictures and notice where they look. Babies turn toward complex patterns such as stripes with high contrast—not simple patterns with little contrast. For example, they love checkerboards and bull's-eyes. Babies also notice the differences between the brightness and texture of two surfaces and where objects begin and end. So, they can identify edges, allowing them to separate different objects (65).

Babies also learn from watching things move, which provides more clues about where things begin and end than edges alone. Even young babies can follow the movements of an object right in front of them. Remarkably, they also seem to be able to predict where an object will move in the future.

In an experiment, a ball was rolling and rolled behind a screen. The baby, who was watching, expected to see the ball come out from the screen's other side. If the ball never emerged, the baby looked even longer and more intently to the edge of the screen— where the ball should have gone.

Or, she even looked on the path the ball should have taken. It's as if she was able to predict where the ball should be if it rolled behind the screen, if it rolled beyond it, and when it should get there (67). Babies also seem to discriminate between a ball that is close up or far away, as well as when an even bigger ball is close and far. In other words, they understand size constancy (68)!

Babies can discriminate between different emotions on people's faces and hear the different voice tones that correspond with them, such as happy, sad, and angry. By one year, they discriminate people from objects and look to their mothers as a reference to know what to prefer and what to reject. For example, if a grown-up looks into two boxes and shows a happy face when she looks in one and a disgusted face at the other, the baby will prefer the box with the happy expression linked to it. The baby doesn't only recognize the grown-up feels happy or disgusted, but also that she *feels* this about something in particular.

Additionally, one-year-old babies can remember past actions and imitate them. For example, when an experimenter touched the top of a box to his forehead, it lit up. The baby could watch but not touch the object. One week later the babies were given the same box, and they instantly touched their foreheads to the top of the box (33–34). How memory is working so early on is fantastic.

If we jump from understanding how the newborn can play with us (with imitating tongue movements) to how the one-year-old can play with us (by remembering and imitating), it's amazing how much goes on in those first twelve months. We can conclude—if we use our imaginations just a bit—that *babies at one year understand others' minds*!

They know what to do with an object by watching us with the object and how to feel about something by seeing how we feel by watching our expressions and observing our postures—all without knowing language.

One-year-olds even know how to point to something they want in order to clearly suggest to the adult to get it for them; they are now communicating with the adult about things that aren't spurred on by their physiological needs.

Further, they know the difference between physical and psychological causality, meaning they can cause an effect on an object differently than they can cause an effect in you. How far they've come in their first year!

By reading all the great experiments researchers do all over the world, you begin to realize how important all those observers think YOU are to your baby. They want you to know that all you do with your baby enhances their development. So, by reading about this fascinating research, you will become an expert, too, with your specific unique baby whom you love! You will understand how and why to choose to play in different ways during different months. How proud you can be not only of your baby but also of yourself as his or her parent.

Month by month, you'll read about the relationship between research experiments, infant development, and various types of play. This will be followed by a written and drawn illustration of a mother or father playing with a baby each month. Also added for further insight is a play session I will describe that depicts my role as an infant-parent psychotherapist playing with a baby and a new young parent. You will be able to enter their world and compare it to your own with your baby month by month from birth to one year.

Now, it's time to play!

Many Meanings of Play

We can't overemphasize the value of play and enjoying play without any agenda. Playing is simply what babies do! They *need* play, both with you and on their own from the very start of their lives.

So, what do we mean by *play*? Play is any activity that focuses on what mothers and fathers and other caregivers are doing as they interact with their babies. Picture your newborn playing when he is lying on his back on your knees. He looks up at you and turns his glance to your voice because you move your lips.

Some babies may even play "possum." How? Well, you may notice when one eye is open and the other is closed. He's alert to happenings in his immediate environment but, at the same time, cleverly not revealing *all* that he is aware of—even in his first few days.

Playing is your baby's way of enjoying himself—and his way of enjoying you! After learning to recognize your voice, face, and touch and associating them with comfort, your baby responds more and more to the fun of playing, even giving you a special treat—his smile!

But what is the meaning and importance of play?

Play Space

Play takes place in the space between the mother and baby—even before the baby clearly knows she is a separate being from the mother. Winnicott calls this space between mother and baby the *potential space* (1971). The potential space is the arena of creativity between the baby and the mother where play takes place.

Play develops the baby's mind. It is a wonderful way to move your baby developmentally forward. This is the pleasure of both mothers and fathers and any primary caregiver who spends a great deal of time with the baby. While mothers are often described as "preoccupied" with their babies, fathers are described as "engrossed" (Ammaniti and Trentini 2009, 541–542). These are fathers who actively play with their babies and are sensitive to the messages their babies communicate through gestures, crying, cooing, and body language, all of which develop the baby's mind.

Meanings of Play

In order to understand the meanings of play, it's important and exciting to understand the inner mental processes that underlie your babies' play. There is no formal recipe, simply a look into your infant's inner world by careful observation. This is what researchers around the world do all the time—they observe carefully. As a parent, you can enjoy observing, too. Every parent can be an expert on their unique baby.

So, do you wonder, *why do babies play?*

Through repetitious play, the baby makes sense of his experiences, current feelings, and desires. He masters what he experiences, and—through the creativity of play—he reviews, advances, retreats, and conquers old and new learning.

There are multiple roles that play has for babies:

- Play communicates, expresses, and represents the baby's experiences.

- Play is a window into the baby's strengths and challenges.

- Play reveals the pleasures as well as the special seriousness with which babies interact with others.

- Play is used for learning to enjoy oneself as well as to cope with distress, conflict, and trauma.

- Play has the power to move development forward and enables babies to both explore and discover new possibilities, as well as communicate when they are overstimulated.

Babies play to learn, to interact, to socialize, to develop fine and gross motor coordination, and—most importantly—to discover their relationship with you, their primary caregiver.

As a parent, *do not* underestimate your capacity to see exchanges with your baby from *his* point of view. Notice how newborns have the capacity to imitate the actions they see on your face such as smiling or sticking the tongue out. Newborns can reproduce facial expressions as part of relationship building. This is all part of play.

As Ammaniti and Trentini (2009) highlight, there is a kind of mutual coordination between a mother and her infant. Together they modulate the timing, the form, and the intensity of their emotional expressions as they interact (554). You might compare this to a dance as mother and infant move and interact together in time.

As you may have noticed, repetition is a driving force behind a baby's play. Babies re-experience pleasure and learning opportunities as they develop along their own timeline and master their abilities and the environment.

Play can be understood as a gradual reworking—over and over—of assimilating piecemeal experiences that are too large to be assimilated in one fell swoop. For example, you may notice how your baby's inexperience in the world makes him vulnerable to overstimulation. At the same time, you may notice when he is flexible in his responses.

For instance, when a mother is interested in playing with a puppet with her baby for an extended period of time hoping to delight him, she may notice after a while instead of a smiling response, the baby averts his head. He averts his head to reduce overstimulation. It is a healthy coping mechanism not at all to be confused with rejecting his mother. If the mother is in tune with this response of reducing stimulation and does not interfere with the baby averting his head to regulate himself, she will then notice in a few moments he turns back to her for further play. Her empathic patience for his need to take a break returns him to a more flexible place to play again, perhaps with something new.

Anna Freud (1965) discovered that the baby's earliest play with his mother's body promotes the infant's capacity for defining himself as a separate self from others. She viewed play as a source of information about the baby's development—a window into the infant's attempts to gain mastery in his environment. Early on the baby is learning the differences between various aspects of reality as his body and his mother's body are used for learning.

Winnicott (1968) also referred to the special role of the body in infant play. He points out that play is pleasurable, but if it is too stimulating then play is disrupted as in the puppet play example. He highlights that play reflects the infant's capacity to understand the differences between what his internal mind can enjoy compared with what external reality might demand. Your infant gradually reworks his world as he plays!

Even young babies use play and other experiences to develop a sense of self as they interact with you. Motor skills, language, and brain and social development increase as they practice and mature. Play promotes growth and assists babies in preparing for future abilities and challenges in each new developmental phase. Even the infant's earliest manipulations of his and her mother's body are indeed, play.

Infantile activities offer pleasure while also giving a beginning orientation to the world (Solnit, Cohen, and Neubauer 1993). They provide the baby's beginning experiences of me and not-me.

Parents and Play

Your parenting activities support and expand your baby's play. In an important sense, parents need to be able to regress or become more like a child to reach to the developmental stages of their infants. This will enable both parent and baby to reach their full creative potential.

In *The Many Meanings of Play: A Psychoanalytic Perspective* Mahon says, "If the parent is to be empathic and effective as a caretaker of children throughout their developmental cycles, he or she must revive the play mode that was temporarily rejected in the service

of other more adult modes of being and thinking and believing"
(1993, 231). Your creative parental playing is essential for your
baby's development. It may take you back to feeling like a kid
again yourself, but this is what your baby needs if you are to play
with him and understand his world.

Transitional Objects

Parents often find that special objects comfort their baby as she
settles for a nap, observes her environment, or plays. These objects
are referred to as transitional objects. It is important for the parent
to understand the importance of these objects as they play with
their baby.

> A fascinating subject of parent participation in play is . . .
> the first "not-me" object, which may be the infant's own
> fingers, the edge of a blanket, or a toy or doll offered by
> the mother for soothing. The infant makes use of objects
> that are not part of the infant's body yet are not fully rec-
> ognized as belonging to external reality. Winnicott termed
> these transitional objects. (Ritvo 1993, 235)

In other words, the maturing baby realizes that her mommy
and daddy may not always be available, so she becomes attached
to a transitional comfort object as a sort of stand-in. It is neither
perceived as internal or external but something in between or
intermediate. Like her parents, the object offers a comfort—particularly when the baby is frustrated, sick, tired, exploring new areas,
or making transitions of any kind. This object is so extraordinary
because it is in the infant's control. It may be voluntarily given up
between ages two and five, but often not until it is lost, falls apart,

or becomes in some way unavailable. In the meantime, it relieves separation anxiety. (See the chapter on the twelfth month.)

As Ritvo states, transitional objects can be something as simple as the satin edge of a blanket, a teddy bear, a nappy, a burp cloth, or whatever stands for the mother in her absence. These transitional objects help babies maneuver their understanding of the mother as both different from them, yet part of their inner world. A mother who fosters and appreciates her baby's attachment to his transitional object (which happens approximately during the ninth month) helps her infant move forward developmentally during the first year.

Pacing Yourself with Your Baby

While growing into your role as a parent as you play with your baby, you need to be patient and relaxed—whether your baby is four or eight months old. Your baby is sensitive to whether you have time and patience for him. Even busy adults in a hurry can be calm and relaxed for the few minutes they are available.

Sometimes maintaining a calm demeanor is easier said than done. However, try to capture the emotional tone of your infant. It can be difficult at times to resist the natural tendency to think your infant's emotional state is like your own. But, adults in play need to identify with their baby—letting your baby know she is understood as she is.

How do we do this? Words are helpful, because a baby recognizes his mother's voice, and the infant will resonate with his mother's way of looking at him or the tone and rhythm of her voice. In play, it's best when the parent tries to convey a sense of emotional warmth instead of challenging the baby. We need to be aware of our own states of mind—be it warmth, anger, irritability, or being overwhelmed. These feelings determine how well we can tune into our baby's emotional state. As mentioned above, do your best to be attending and engaging at your baby's pace.

Some parents, especially parents of their first newborn, are understandably anxious as they are experiencing a tiny baby for the first time. Babies and parents, however, can slowly learn to adapt to each other's rhythms and tempos if they are patient and observant. How does a mother become truly aware of her baby? She learns how her individual baby takes in information and responds to all sensory modalities such as sound, touch, smell, and vision. She learns to capture her baby's emotional tone with a sense of connectedness that helps the baby attend. The sight, sound, smell, touch, and movement of a mother's body affects how she actively facilitates her baby's development. This takes time, patience, and a lot of repetition. Mothers can observe, learn, and try different ways of engaging as they fine-tune their approach to playing with their unique baby.

Responding to Baby's Senses

In the first weeks of a baby's life, the mother begins to learn how her infant responds to different sensory modalities—sight, sound, smell, and touch. She begins to question how her specific baby responds to loud noise and if she has a child who prefers soft and gentle sounds. Some babies are frightened by loud sounds; others tune out sounds that are too soft. The mother also notes if her baby likes bright lights or soft lights.

Does your baby like a lot to be going on when she's fully awake or does she move at a slower pace? Does your baby like you to be animated and use hand gestures? Does he like bright colors and a lot of detail as he develops his curiosity? Or, does he like simple, slow movements rather than complex and rapid changes? As you become a keen observer of your baby, you will notice the differences.

Notice your baby's response to touch. She may crave touch or avoid it. The irritable baby may be one who craves touch. Another infant may crave touch through light tickling and then want more roughhousing when she gets older.

Does your infant relax when gently touched on the hand or shoulder? Or, does he stiffen up when approached too quickly and feel disturbingly surprised by a quick, casual, light touch? The infant who doesn't like a light touch may like firm pressure, like a warm bear hug. In fact, the baby who doesn't respond easily to touch may actually need a lot of touching. These are all things you can figure out as you observe and learn with your baby.

Mothers need to avoid preconceptions about their babies throughout the first twelve months. In each mode of sensory development, a child can be hyperreactive (that is, very sensitive) or hyporeactive (less sensitive) and may crave more of a particular sensation. Is your baby hyper- or hyposensitive to a particular mode of input, such as sight, sound, taste, touch, movement, or smell? Does your baby seek extra movement or avoid it? Your infant is even communicating these wide range of needs by how he mouths her fingers and toes, or by relaxing or tensing up his muscles. Observing how your baby responds to the world will give you all sorts of clues as to what he enjoys or needs.

Some babies crave movement and others are more easily startled. Your infant's sensory responses indicate the role his physical makeup will play as he is engaged and attends to play. An animated adult can mistakenly overwhelm a baby. Alternatively, a baby who is under-reactive to sensory experiences may not respond to a soft, gentle mother who speaks very quietly. The under-reactive baby needs someone to be more energetic and active by sounding excited to rev up her infant to keep him engaged by pulling him in.

Trying to connect with your baby through all his sensory modalities can enhance his sense of emotional security, bringing pleasure and intimacy to both mother and infant, a warmly connected pair.

To tie in a principle that was stated earlier, the mother needs to not only attend to the baby's sensory modalities (sight, sound, smell, and touch) but to her pace. Some babies—even when they crave a lot of input—may be slow to bond, whereas others are quick to form relationships. Some babies' gazes take longer to find their mothers' eyes. A four-month-old baby may take twenty or thirty seconds, rather than five seconds, to tune in. In these cases, mothers who give up at fifteen seconds may never discover their babies' capacities to tune-in (Greenspan 1997). This two-way communication may seem overwhelming, but you can readily adapt to your baby with joy and elation as she plays—it might just take some trial and error. Be patient with yourself and your baby.

Communication with Your Baby

Eventually, play involves two-way communication. Emotional gesturing—such as experimenting with smiling at a smiling baby or frowning or smiling at a frowning baby—is natural for many mothers. Others need to learn by practice which is just fine.

Emotional gesturing with infants involves facial expressions, hand and arm movement, body posture, and slow or excited voice tones. Gazing, simply looking in your baby's eyes and allowing or encouraging her to return your gaze, is also a part of facial expression that involves two-way engagement. Awareness of these subtle aspects of communication enhances your ability to engage your baby and bond early on. However, it's essential to let your baby be the leader; she is the boss! According to Greenspan (1997), the mother picks up her pace and can enliven it or dampen it depending on how the baby reacts. Knowing when to not intrude or when to reach out is important. This is learned by observing your baby's reactions as she grows.

The following ideas supporting a mother's ability to change with her infant—beginning even in pregnancy—can add more insight and hope to these attempts to observe your infant's reactions.

First, let's think about fascinating hormonal and neurochemical systems in each mother that prepares her for her role with her baby.

Striking changes occur in the maternal brain that enable her to respond to her infant from the start. It is helpful to understand that the regulation of maternal behavior involves the coordination of many hormonal and neurochemical systems. That is, the female brain is especially responsive to the changes that occur during pregnancy. In particular, the hormones vasopressin and oxytocin (Insel and Young 2001) stimulate bonding between a mother and her infant.

Besides hormones, other chemicals affecting the nervous system also play a role in triggering maternal responses. For example, endorphins prepare the mother for the discomfort of delivery and may initiate maternal behavior. (Ammaniti and Trentini 2009, 548).

How do we know what is happening to the new mother's brain that naturally is assisting her in understanding her baby's emotional reactions? Using brain imaging, it has been found that the right orbitofrontal cortex (in the front of the brain behind the eye sockets) moderates the mother's abilities to understand her infant's emotional cues and then respond to them sensitively (Nitschke et al. 2004).

Do you as a mother feel your natural yearning to play with your baby? This is because, as just noted, the mother is *biologically* programmed from her pregnancy to want to play with her infant during the first few days and that important first month. Her biology is getting her prepared for what's to come in her soon-to-be-discovered play with her baby infant. This innate biology solves the mystery of why the mother is equipped to play actively from day one!

Have you noticed a natural tendency to hold your baby in a certain way as a mother? Did you know that this is because mothers are innately geared to give comfort to their infants? How do we know this? Through observation it's been found that both right- and left-handed mothers hold their babies with the left side of their body. They are innately, biologically programmed to do so.

In fact, you may notice how mothers use their left arms and hands more often than fathers and nonmothers. Why? What does this do? It puts the infant on the left side of the mother's vision that is actually communicating with her right hemisphere. Sound complicated? Well, it's that right hemisphere that produces natural comforting gestures (Schore 2003; Sieratzki and Woll 1996).

It's intriguing to learn how the left side of the body communicates with the right hemisphere of the brain, but mothers don't have to know this, they just do it. For example, the way a mother snuggles her baby comfortably in her left arm naturally soothes her baby. It is truly amazing how without trying, mothers innately give the comforting gestures their babies need!

According to Ainsworth (1967), "Attachment is more than an overt behavior, it is internal" (429). What does that mean? Something inside the mother naturally leads her to form an attachment to her baby that leads to their bonding.

No wonder the mother is adapted for play with her newborn! If you feel like playing with your baby, it's just what you are naturally geared for. Enjoy these playful feelings. Now let's see what you can do in each and every month of the first year with your enchanting baby.

Stimulus Seeking
by Your Baby

What Do Researchers Have to Say about Your One-Month-Old?

It used to be thought that a newborn could not distinguish one thing from another. It was believed that she could not distinguish an external thing from her own body and that she did not experience the environment as separate from herself. If this were true, how would we answer the question, "Does the baby perceive the breast as part of herself?"

Early researchers like Rene Spitz (1965) thought that in the first weeks, the outside world was practically nonexistent for infants. Today we question this. Recent research has demonstrated that from birth infants are capable of what is called a *primary social relatedness* (Beebe 2014). This means that from birth the baby wants to relate to you, their primary caregiver. Experimenters like Meltzoff

(1990) have even discovered that "as early as forty-two minutes after birth, infants can imitate gestures of others" (Beebe, Cohen, and Lachmannn 2016, 13). Can you imagine? Just forty-two minutes after delivery your infant wants to imitate you! How is it that these experimenters discovered this incredible finding?

They discovered that infants perceive similarities, or what experimenters called correspondences, between their own behaviors and the behaviors they see the experimenter perform. For example, the experimenter may open his mouth and thrust out his tongue. As the infant watches the experimenter do this for about a minute while this baby has a pacifier in her mouth, ever so slowly, after the pacifier is removed, the baby's face matches this facial movement of the experimenter and gradual imitates what she sees (13–14).

It has also been repeatedly observed that from the start that newborns seek stimuli naturally. They show rooting, sucking, molding, and orienting. They also track moving objects visually. The most exciting moving object they track, of course, is you, their parent's face.

As your baby gazes at you, you may see your infant widen her eyes and show subtle facial expressions. Your little one wants to seek and even initiate social play. However, she may also need to modify the degree of social stimulation seen in the faces before her, so she is not overwhelmed. If you are making too many different faces or being very animated that may stimulate her too much; she may just need a break. When this happens, she will initiate *self-quieting measures* such as averting her head or closing her eyes (Beebe, Cohen, and Lachmann 2016, 13).

Remarkably, and much earlier than was first thought, your infant can not only match your external behavior but also capture the quality of your *internal* feelings. Your baby feels if you are sad, happy, excited, or relaxed.

Further, from birth infants are motivated to identify patterns, orders, and sequences in behaviors they see as events over time. Babies are called *contingency detectors* from birth. A contingency refers to how babies can identify if one thing happens, another will follow. That is, they don't have to be taught to detect "if-then patterns and sequences" (Beebe et al. 2010, 14). An example of this is when your baby opens her mouth and it's followed by your smile. When this sequence is repeated a few times, it is now predictable for the infant. Your infant comes to expect your smile. She expects her action, opening her mouth, results in your smile.

That is, the two of you are interacting and your baby has come to expect this beginning connection with you. This is the if-then pattern or sequence. It is truly startling that it used to be thought that newborns could not distinguish one thing from another when now we know they can even expect how one thing (such as what they do) leads to another (what you do in response).

However, you will notice that each newborn differs in several ways such as in their temperaments, sleep patterns, feeding schedules, arousal patterns, and sensitivities to sound, smell, or touch. Some infants can dampen (lessen) their arousal and inhibit their behavior if they feel overstimulated. This may show as an infant turns away or begins to look sleepy.

In fact, it is amazing how even *before* birth, some fetuses in the last trimester have "the capacity to put [themselves] to sleep in the face of repeated light flashes or sounds." This leads to differing abilities to self-regulate (calm themselves down) after birth (Brazelton 1992, 15). So, your baby is actually learning to respond to the outside environment and soothe herself in utero—before you even meet each other face-to-face!

Jumping ahead quite a bit to see what's to come, at approximately five months old, babies begin to experience a gradual—but significant—mental separation. That is an understanding of their boundaries as an individual. Thus, you as the mother or father are increasingly viewed as an individual, separate from the baby. Before this leap takes place, how do mothers and fathers play with their infants to foster their development? Let's take a look first at their development and then their play.

Infant Development

Speech

Daniel Stern, MD, a pioneer in infant research, believes that infants are *stimulus-seeking* (1985, 183). That is, your infant needs to be brought to a particular level of stimulation and then maintained at that level—both appropriate to whatever stage she is in. For example, you may gently pat her tummy and speak in a sing-song *motherese* high-pitched voice and see her eyes sparkle in response and the corners of her lips turn up in recognition. She feels your tenderness on her tummy and recognizes your voice becoming more alert, even animated. How different this is from a view from the past that infants are essentially inactive and somnolent most of the time. Stern's research teaches us the following:

- From the first day of life, the baby pursues others with their sight and sounds.

- There are strong preferences from the beginning for certain stimuli, such as facial expressions, speech sounds, and tonal ranges at particular pitches.

- The baby has discriminatory capabilities. The mother, for example, can be distinguished from a stranger by two weeks simply by listening to her.

- A baby's interest in speech sounds can overpower the baby's interest in food, even when the baby is hungry.

- By four weeks, the infant can discriminate "Ba" and "Pa" sounds.

- Baby talk is characterized by long pauses and by short verbalizations. This is recommended rather than adult talk because baby talk facilitates the processing or adaptation of the baby to the speech of others that is optimal for him.

- There are paraverbal or musical expressions of speech sounds. In other words, it is not what is said, but how it is said that secures and maintains attention (184).

- Infants are "predesigned to seek out and engage in learning opportunities" (Stern 1985, 46).

Stern also shows the progression of maternal speech over a baby's first year and its optimal effects at different age points. From birth to two months of age, the timing and rhythm of maternal speech naturally seems to be what is most effective (1985, 184).

However, by six months old, the tone of voice and tonal variations are most important. Then, by the end of the baby's first year, grammar begins to enter the picture. From here your baby learns sounds, words, and even ideas at an amazing rate. So, we see your newborn has an exciting road ahead of him and that play with talking will help him to eventually begin to speak!

Actually, babies know a lot about language right off the bat. Being exposed to a specific language fine-tunes their brains and shapes their minds, so babies perceive sounds differently in different countries.

Here's a fascinating experiment that tells us about how babies discriminate different sounds. If you give a baby a special nipple that is connected to a computer, she can tell us what she hears by her sucking. That is, instead of producing milk by sucking, the baby's sucking on this device produces sounds from a loudspeaker—one sound per each hard suck.

Babies may suck up to eighty times a minute to keep the sound turned on until they get bored. At one month old, babies in this study could discriminate every English sound contrast given to them.

For example, when American infants listened, they thought all the r's were the same and different from all the l's—just like an adult (Gopnik, Meltzoff, and Kuhl 1999, 105). Even more exciting, however, was that these American babies discriminated sounds from different languages, including those they'd never heard before! This means that babies learning language sounds outperform their parents who have already filtered out sounds that don't correspond to their native language.

Sight

Early on a baby's behavior, specifically gaze regulation (eye contact or lack of it), can change a mother's mood. Stern (1985) points out that an infant can see as well as an adult certainly by three months and probably long before. That is, the infant has the same amount of control over the visual system as an adult has by three months old. This is in contrast to the other systems, which are relatively immature. So, at three months a baby can see his world as well as you but certainly cannot yet explore his world in other ways as you do.

How does the infant's use of vision affect their parent's behavior? Young infants use the center of their field of vision where visual acuity is at its highest to regulate gazing at or away from others. Looking at or away from a mother has a powerful effect on the mother's behavior. This illustrates the exquisite control an infant has over what he will or will not take in and how he affects his caregiver's behavior. So, if your baby looks away from you, he may simply be reducing stimulation. It's important not to feel personally rejected, because that is not the meaning of his behavior. He likely just wants a little break.

The Relationship between Sight, Sound, and Touch

Play involves learning; it even helps a baby form a sense of self (Stern 1985, 47). The baby first learns with his body, as you interact with his fingers and toes. This also helps him to recognize that something that can be seen, touched, or heard can be the same thing. As your baby sees your smile, hears your voice, and feels your touch he is learning all these sensations are one wonderful person, Mommy.

In an interesting experiment done by Meltzoff and Borton in 1979 described by Stern, babies were blindfolded and given two different pacifiers to suck.

One pacifier had a spherical-shaped nipple and the other was a nipple with nubs protruding from various points around its surface. After the baby had had some experience feeling (touching) the nipple with only the mouth, the nipple was removed and placed side by side with the other kind of nipple. The blindfold was taken off. After a quick visual comparison, infants looked more at the nipple they had just sucked. (Stern 1985, 47–48)

The infant knew that the nipple she had felt was what she now saw. Touch and vision were naturally connected by the baby. Another way to say this is that infants are innately able to transfer information and recognize a tie between touch and vision (48).

This is illustrated when babies recognize different rattles that you put before them that they touch, see, and hear. This is called audio-visual matching. The ability to perform audio-visual matching appears to be well within an infant's capacity by three weeks of age. Amazingly enough, speech itself—in a natural situation—is visual as well as auditory, because the lips move. Understanding goes up considerably when the lips are in view.

According to a study headed by Haith, by six weeks old babies tend to look more closely at faces that speak (Haith, Hazen, and Goodman 1988). Moreover, when an actual sound heard (shaking a rattle, clapping hands, or hitting a drum) is in conflict with lip movements seen ("Oh, baby look!"), the visual information unexpectedly predominates over the auditory. In other words, we hear what we see, not what is said (Stern 1985, 50)!

We can pull these findings together by concluding that infants have an innate ability to have learning experiences across different sensory modalities (Stern 1985, 50–51). That is, as noted above, what is seen or heard by the baby, two sensory modalities, makes a difference in what draws the baby's immediate or first attention. When the baby heard a rattle and saw lips talking at the same time, he pursued what he saw (lips moving) before what he heard (the noise of a rattle).

Movement

What about the sensory modality of movement or motion in the first month? Does a baby have a sensation of his own movement or motion of body parts? According to an experiment by Meltzoff and Moore (1983), three-week-old infants would imitate an adult model in sticking out their tongues and opening their mouths. Thus, there was an innate correspondence between what infants saw and what they moved—their tongues. It was also found that even the protrusion of a pencil or something similar also may produce infant tongue protrusion (702–709).

Some parents don't want to depend on researcher's discoveries. They want to make these discoveries themselves. If you're inclined to be a researcher, you can see how your infant learns before your very eyes. Try these experiments yourself—simply stick out your tongue at your baby or hold out a pencil and see what your baby does! You can become as expert at these experiments as the researchers. As we'll see when we talk about play below, this little experiment becomes a way to play and interact with your baby. Now you know why. It has to do with the baby's learning capacity to use what he sees with his eyes and what he does with his body parts in imitation. It's so exciting and fun when you see your baby imitate you.

Emotions

Sometimes experiments just raise more and more questions.

It was reported that newborn infants, age two days, would reliably imitate an adult model who either smiled, frowned, or showed a surprise face. The problems presented by these findings are manifold. How do babies "know" that they have a face or facial features? How do they "know" that the face they see is anything like the face they have? (Stern 1985)

Additionally, how do they "know" that the faces they are seeing can do what their own faces can? Experiments just can't answer all these fascinating questions about a baby's learning capacities. "Thus, infants cannot know what they do not know, nor that they do not know" (Stern 1985, 46). What about other emotions? It is also believed that babies perceive global emotions, such as happy, sad, or angry (Werner 1948).

Try experimenting with different expressions on your face and see if your baby imitates. What is fascinating is that babies by two months generally visualize first from the perimeter of an object and then to the internal view of the object—except in relation to the face. The sound of your voice shifts the baby's attention to the internal facial features. This is aided by the baby's attraction to the movement of your mouth. So, try and figure out when your baby recognizes you—it could be happening right now, as you read this book in front of her!

Do infants experience pleasure and displeasure in the first months of life? When watching an infant in distress or contentment, it is very hard not to believe this is so. As you experiment with different types of play, notice the expressions on your baby's face and you'll know what to repeat and what to discontinue to make your baby happy. Stern notes that according to Izard (1978), newborns show interest, joy, distress, disgust, and surprise. And these emotions aren't only expressed in the still face; a baby's anger can also be seen in his moving face, arms, and whole body when he experiences a momentary lack of air at the breast. Also, a baby's entire body reveals pleasure during the quivering of his beginning smiles (Stern 1985, 66).

> We simply do not know if infants are actually feeling what their faces, voices, and bodies so powerfully express to us, but it is very hard to witness such expressions and not to make that inference. . . . They need the feelings they express to regulate themselves, to define their very selves, and to learn with. (Stern 1985, 66)

With all of this information, we discern that infants' feelings are, indeed, what they are actually showing us. Visual contact is central to a baby's emotional attachment to her mother. In fact, from the beginning, mother and baby coordinate their "eye-to-eye orientations, vocalizations, hand gestures, and movements of the arms and head" to express their emotions to each other (Trevarthen and Aitken 2001, 3–48).

So, how do babies regulate their emotions, so they are not overstimulated or overwhelmed, and how do their mothers help them do this? Mothers and babies mutually regulate (manage and modulate) their emotional interactions naturally at an optimal range to which the baby can adapt. For example, if the baby fusses a bit as a form of communication that he is hungry, the mother responds by understanding this communication and nurses her baby. Or, if the baby rubs his eyes signaling he is tired, the mother holds him and rocks him until she sees it's time for a nap. This is the way mothers and babies adjust to and modify each other's behavior. Alternatively, in play, the baby adapts to his mother's face when she may exaggerate or vary her emotional expressions more than ordinarily. When baby sees his mommy's big eyes and smile, he increases his gaze and broadens his smile enjoying the interplay.

It is easier to see how mothers and babies react positively to each other regulating each other's behavioral responses when they are feeling good and enjoying each other's emotions and understanding their communications as they play. But some mothers who are more drawn to unsettling emotions may, unfortunately, be mostly or nearly only responsive when they see or even cause their baby distress. These babies will still interact, because they yearn for attention from their mothers and want it even when it's only under negative circumstances. Therefore, if the mother causes harm to her baby or sees he is in distress, and that is primarily when she will give her attention, the baby will learn that is when she responds. Sadly, if he learns that when he is hurt in some way, that's when he gets more of a reaction from his mother than when he feels joy, he will become more alert to those situations.

If you find that you are more alert to your child's distress than pleasurable experiences and respond mostly at those times, perhaps you and your child will be missing out on enjoying each other in ways to benefit you both. In order to have more pleasure as a mother and for your baby to feel more secure, you may wish to take the opportunity to discuss how you and your baby interact as you play with a mental health professional especially trained to guide mothers and fathers with their infants. This will not only increase your knowledge of play with your baby, but also give you a closer bond that you can build on in the future. Pediatricians offer such referrals that you can depend on.

What Is Me or Not-Me

Now we can return to the question I asked at the beginning: Does the infant *know* the breast is not part of herself?

According to Stern's conclusions (1985, 52), the breast would be instinctively placed in the "not part of myself" category because *the breast as seen and the breast as sucked will be understood as a separate entity by the baby!* Who would have thought that the baby has such a fine-tuned perception as he breastfeeds? Or does he? You can speculate on your own!

Facial Recognition

Facial recognition by the baby of the mother is fascinating. Two- to three-day-old infants discriminate and imitate smiles, frowns, and surprise expressions seen on the face of the person they are interacting with. By one month, infants enjoy an animated human face as a whole, not just specific features. This is why the evidence is convincing that newborns discriminate their mothers' voices from other's voices reading the same material, because they do not only remember their particular mother's voice but also recognize her face at the same time according to Stern (1985) who references Donee (1973). Infants also gaze differently at the human face than at objects that have geometric forms or inanimate patterns. They move their arms and legs and open and close their hands and feet in smoother, more regulated, less jerky cycles of movement and emit more vocalizations when scanning live faces according to Beebe (2000) who cites Field et al. (1983) and DeCasper and Fifer (1980).

There is some debate about exactly how early a baby recognizes individual faces prior to two months. Many researchers continue to find it, but a larger number do not (Lamb and Sherrod 1981). Still, it is clear that young infants enjoy looking into their parent's eyes, hearing their voices, and responding with movement and facial expressions. As you play with your baby, you will learn how your baby specifically responds to your facial expressions.

There is little question that infants construct and perceive relationships with others directly (Stern 1985, 63–64). This shows us that babies want to relate to you; that is, they want to play! Whatever kind of play you experiment with, your baby's facial recognition of you will be a priority for her. You are relating to your infant through your play and there is a relationship forming. How exciting!

With all of this information, we must discern that infants' feelings are, indeed, what they are actually showing us. Visual contact is central to a baby's attachment to her mother. In fact, from the beginning mother and baby coordinate their "eye-to-eye orientations, vocalizations, hand gestures, and movements of the arms and head" to express their emotions to each other (Trevarthen and Aitken 2001, 3–48).

I hope that this all encourages you to play with your baby— even in the first month. He is mentally and physically ready to watch, listen, learn from, and enjoy your face, emotions, and so much more. Follow your baby's cues, and you'll be able to enjoy communicating with your one-month-old—and both of you will learn as you interact.

Playtime Suggestions

How is play behavior related to these research findings? Even in the first month your baby can *play* as you creatively gaze, vocalize, and hold her in different positions. Play is focused on the body—or what might be called the body-self that is emerging. This is play because it is stimulating. It is important, however, to notice when your baby gets tired and overstimulated—which will happen quickly in babies so young. You can tell that your baby is tired or overstimulated when she looks away or her body turns away. When you notice this, it is time to let your infant (and you!) rest.

Let's think about the first few days. It is thought that most babies want action as soon as they are awake (Van de Rijt, Plooij, and Plas-Plooij 2019, 57). Your baby can lift his head briefly when on his tummy; move his arms and legs on both sides of his body equally well; and focus on objects that are within eight to fifteen inches away from his face. At this stage, play is simply how you are interacting with your baby. Spend time skin to skin; this can also mean holding your infant close to your chest while you feed or cuddle him. Stroke and massage your infant. Look into your baby's eyes and smile. In a short time, he'll start to mimic your expressions and smile spontaneously.

Remember that although babies distinguish voices, they do so only one at a time, so keep other sounds off. Talk to your baby by cooing, babbling, singing, and speaking to him; he loves the sound of your voice, as he remembers it from when he was in utero. In fact, when your baby hears your unique voice, there may already be a sense of "we" between mother and baby.

It takes about three to four weeks, but around this time a baby will be able to focus on a mobile as more than a blur. This can be another early way to help your baby to play. Place a mobile eight to fifteen inches away, and she will begin to enjoy examining it. Keep in mind that a mobile can be beneficial hung to either side of the crib as well as above, as infants tend to look from side to side and not just straight above when lying in their cribs.

Although your baby doesn't see you as a separate person quite yet, this doesn't mean you cannot play with him! As mentioned above, your baby enjoys looking at things, and you can begin to show him plenty of visual stimuli—as long as you don't overload him.

Keep these things in mind as you find objects for your baby to stare at:

- One or two eye-catching objects at a time are about all your baby can handle at this age.

- Babies have short attention spans, so change activities frequently.

- Babies prefer to gaze at things with sharp contrasts, so find things that are black and white or red and yellow.

- Babies love looking at small lights, so you might take a pen flashlight and move it slowly for your infant to follow.

- Babies love looking at bright objects like a lamp or a window with vertical or horizontal blinds.

- Babies prefer a well-lit room to a dim one (Murkoff, Eisenberg, and Hathaway 2003).

An Illustration of a Mother and One-Month-Old Baby at Play

Sometimes it feels a little funny to talk and play with your infant, especially when you are new to each other. What do you say?

Here is an example of some things you may say or experience with your baby.

Mommy: "Hi, Sweetie. Ooh. Look at me smile. Ah, you like that. I see it in your twinkling eyes. Ooh. Here's a frown. Oh my. That looks different. I'll smile again, you little cutie."

Baby is making eye contact, watching Mommy's lips move as she speaks and seems cheerfully attentive.

Mommy: "Ooh. I know. It's time to change your diaper. I heard you poop. Good one, Sweetie. Okay, let's change that diaper. Let's make you nice and clean. That's good. And now some crème. Oh. You're all fixed up. I'm going to hold you close against my skin before we put your diaper on."

Baby loves this snuggle. She makes little sounds of pleasure.

Mommy: "Now it's time to nurse. Okay let's sit here so comfy together. Oh, I love you so much."

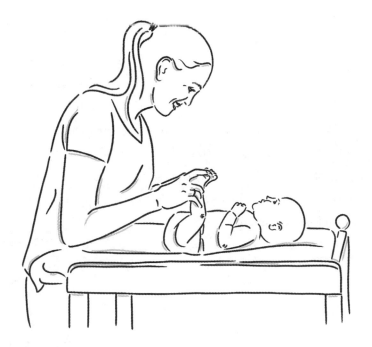

A PLAY SESSION

I remember playing with twenty-one-year-old Lara and her one-month-daughter in their small home. Very inexperienced as a new mother with no one to guide her, Lara complains her baby is "fussing" a lot. She says to me she has been fed but keeps crying on and off. I notice that Lara has a rather rushed manner, pushing the bottle again and again into her baby's mouth, but the infant isn't interested. She shows this by turning her head away. I hope Lara doesn't feel rejected, so I watch even more carefully.

I see Lara all too quickly pick up her baby and pace rapidly around the room holding her tightly. The fast movement and tight hold I think to myself might be too stimulating. Frustrated, Lara lays her back on the bed and asks me to watch her for a few minutes.

"Sure," I say. "Take a break."

When she leaves the room for a moment and I am alone with the infant on the bed lying on her back, I quietly and slowly say, "So how are you doing, little one?"

My slow approach immediately stops the crying that Lara had called fussing. I hold up a black-and-white simple drawing on a card of some sheep. The baby wiggles her arms and legs liking the contrasting black-and-white lines.

When Lara returns, she says in astonishment, "Oh. She's so settled now. How'd you do that?"

I don't want Lara to think of me as a better mother than she is, so I simply explain. "Sometimes babies like their mommies to move slowly. It's sooth-ing. Would you like to relax a bit yourself and talk to her?"

Lara replies, "What should I talk about?"

"How about telling her softly what you just did. Say something like Mommy went. . .and tell her where you went."

Lara says picking up on my slow talk, "Baby, Mommy went and turned on the washing machine."

The baby stared wide-eyed at Lara wiggling her toes and opening and closing her fists.

I point out, "See all her toes and fists move? That's because she is enjoying when you are speaking to her."

Lara says, "I did that? It was so easy. I guess I'm tense and have to slow down."

"Sure. It's a strain to be a mother of a one-month-old. She loved when you spoke to her so calmly. That was great. Talking is playing."

Lara: "I didn't think of talking as playing. What else can I do?"

"I see you have these cards with black-and-white drawings. They are great for play. Did you know experts say newborns like simple black-and-white pictures?"

"Oh, I wondered what to do with those. They were a present."

"Try just holding one up that you like and let's see her reaction."

Seeing the card with sheep, Lara holds it up and says, "See the sheep?"

Lara is thrilled. "Oh, look at her getting all excited. Her arms and legs are moving at once. She's staring at the card."

"Now you're just as expert as researchers who found out babies like black and white."

"I am? That's really good. You think I can be an expert with *my* baby?"

"Sure. You just showed yourself you can. Your baby's still happy, moving about. Like you said before her arms and legs are moving at once. She plays like that because she's happy. Pick out another card you like."

She picks out a black-and-white picture of a house and trees.

"Look at the house and the big trees. Do you like this, too?" asks Lara.

Lara is grinning at me. "I feel so much better. She likes what I'm doing. I don't have to keep trying to feed her. I kept thinking that only sucking made her stop fussing. She likes to play, and it's so simple."

I reply, "What a happy Mommy you are when you play with your baby. You know, I don't think her fussing is a problem. I think she's trying to tell you she just needs something else. It's her way of talking to you. She's smart. Fussing is just her way of talking."

"Fussing is talking? No one ever told me that before," says Lara. "I even think this is fun. She's still staring at the card and . . . at me!"

"I'd say she likes you!"

Lara smiles at me, feeling much calmer herself, which of course also calms her baby.

What Does Lara Discover
Playing with Her Baby?

Lara learns quickly how her baby is communicating to her at this early stage of development and how using research helps her know what kinds of play her baby enjoys while she, too, is enjoying her baby's response to her choice of activities. As a mother she's learned she has an impact on her baby's behavior and her baby's behavior has an impact on her. In this brief hour, Lara feels more confident as a mother; her tension is reduced considerably, which eases her baby's reactions to her; and she is finding that play can be both vocal, by talking, as well as visual, by using an inanimate object like the black-and-white card.

You, too, will enjoy communicating with your baby at this early stage of development. Have you noticed how your baby focuses in on both the visual and auditory aspects of your talking to her? With each day or even each hour, your confidence increases with your new experiences. You can feel proud of your already growing relationship with your baby.

Creating Stimulating Experiences *with* Your Baby

What Do Researchers Have to Say about Your Two-Month-Old?

Now that your baby is two months old, it's time to get to know her even better. While doing so, keep in mind that all babies reach their milestones on their own timeline; your baby's progress is normal for your baby. Premature infants usually reach milestones later than others of the same birth age and act closer to the age of those with the same due date—or sometimes later (Murkoff, Eisenberg, and Hathaway 2003, 212). Other babies simply have characteristics or inclinations to walk or crawl or reach other milestones sooner or later than others.

Five- to six-week-old babies are willing to work hard with you to feel interesting sensations. In an experiment in a lab, babies adjusted the focus of a movie by sucking harder on their pacifier. When the sucking stopped, the picture blurred. Because babies at this age have trouble sucking and watching at once, they kept this up for only a short time, a few seconds. Then, to see if that's what the babies really intended, the researchers altered the experiment so babies had to stop their sucking to bring the picture back into focus, and they could do that as well (Van de Rijt, Plooij, and Plas-Plooij 2019, 93)!

Give babies a chance to respond. Studies have demonstrated that infants whose parents talk *with* them rather than *at* them, as if in a conversation, begin to learn to talk earlier. Pause and give your infant a chance to coo, gurgle, or giggle. In other words, give her a chance to respond as you look into her eyes.

Infant Development

Cognitive

Cognitive development is obviously important for young babies, but what some parents don't realize is that they can help their baby to cognitively develop through *play*. I recommend sitting with your infant and showing him images in picture books. Choose books that contain simple images with contrasting bright colors like black and white and red and yellow. You can also talk to your baby throughout the day and encourage him to interact with his environment by hanging a toy above his crib or play area. Another fun idea is to use an unbreakable mirror in play. This will allow your baby to see his image and begin to develop a sense of self. Select toys for your child that use different sounds and noises. This will help build his curiosity. Babies learn by seeing right from the start, so by two months old they can see quite a lot. They differentiate between inanimate objects and people and between different human beings. They interpret your body language just as you are interpreting theirs.

Physical

Two-month-old babies are slowly gaining more control over their bodies. You may notice your baby holding her head a little steadier while lying on her tummy or being supported upright. You can help this development with play! Give your two-month-old *tummy time* several times a day. The March of Dimes encourages parents to do this by turning a baby onto her tummy and propping her head to avoid suffocation. Be sure your choice of a prop is safe and comfortable. Tummy time develops the muscles in your infant's neck, arms, and shoulders. In addition to tummy time, choose hanging toys for your baby's crib or playpen that feature colorful pieces that will attract your child's interest. When she reaches out to grab them, this action will tone her muscles and help her to develop smooth movements.

In the second month of life, babies continue to have a strong sucking reflex. Your infant may like to suck on his fist or a few fingers. This is one of the best ways a baby can comfort himself—and it's a kind of play!

At two months old, your infant probably doesn't quite have the coordination to play with toys. But she may bat at a colorful object hanging in front of her or even briefly hold a toy that you place in one of her hands. Her senses are beginning to work together to learn about the world, so be sure to provide plenty of sensory-stimulating experiences.

The two-month-old baby averages approximately thirteen hours of sleep—plus dozing time—during each twenty-four-hour day, but your baby needs more than sleep during this important month of development. She is becoming increasingly active and alert, giving the two of you more time for interaction. Infants at this age typically sleep for four to five hours and then wake up for food. This waking period is a time to stimulate your baby's emotional, intellectual, and physical growth. The time can also allow you to guide your child to develop early social skills, like that first real smile! So be sure to provide plenty of sensory-stimulating experiences for your two-month-old.

Other important signs of physical development include when your baby can:

- lift his head forty-five degrees on his stomach

- hold his head steady when upright

- roll over one way

- reach for an object (as little as a raisin, so be sure to keep that out of hand's reach)

- at best, follow an object held approximately six inches above her face moving 180 degrees from one side to the other (Murkoff, Eisenberg, and Hathaway 2003, 212, 223).

Emotional

As mentioned in the chapter on the first month, your baby already has the ability to recognize facial expressions and mimic them. So, don't forget to keep smiling for your baby and encouraging him to smile back when he coos. Model exaggerated facial expressions to show surprise or delight and give your baby an extra big smile to show your enjoyment of him. Your happy face not only demonstrates to your baby that you delight in him, but it also shows him how to use facial expressions in similar situations. See how broadly your baby smiles; do you see the full gape smile yet?

Believe it or not, soothing is a way of emotionally playing with your five-week-old. So, what can you do to soothe your young baby? You may cuddle, caress, rock back and forth, walk slowly, hum, or pat gently on his bottom (Rijt, Plooj, and Plas-Plooij 1992, 92).

You can also give your two-month-old a lot of hugs to show your love, as well as to demonstrate how to show affection. The National Center for Infants, Toddlers, and Families tells parents that it's impossible to spoil a two-month-old by giving too much affection. Hug and kiss away!

Social

One of the best things you can do for your baby's social development is *talk*. Begin to talk to your baby frequently in several ways.

1. Narrate a running commentary on all that you are doing. For example, when you are putting on a diaper, tell your baby what you are doing. When you put her T-shirt on, say that you're putting it over her head and sliding it down. Tell her when you are fastening her overalls. When you're in the kitchen preparing her bottle, describe what you are doing. During the bath, do the same thing. Explain about soap and rinsing and that her shampoo makes her hair clean and glossy. It doesn't matter that your baby doesn't understand all your details, she is interested in hearing your voice and learning how to listen.

2. Ask babies questions before they have the answers! For example, ask them which T-shirt they like better, the yellow or the red? When shopping, ask if you should buy the sweet or tart baby food. You may be surprised when one day, you get a cooing answer!

3. Consciously use simple phrases that your baby will learn to recognize in time, such as "Bye-bye," "Here are your toes," and "Look at your fingers move."

4. Babies don't understand pronouns, so use the name you are thinking of, like "Mommy is here to play" and "Daddy is going to change the diaper."

5. Raise your pitch, because babies *usually* prefer a high-pitched voice. Watch for your infant's reaction when you do so. Some babies prefer a lower pitch—in fact, daddy's voice may be quite soothing. Experiment, watch, and learn.

6. Focus on the here and now so that your baby hears words that match what he can see or feel.

7. Imitate your baby's sounds and even exaggerate them. When she coos, coo back. When she says, "Ahh," repeat it again and again. Imitating language is a game your infant will enjoy. Plus, it builds self-esteem because you're demonstrating that what she says matters.

8. Sing what you have to say. Singing adds rhythm and varying pitches and tones to language. It even instills social development by adding stimulating language. Use

hand gestures while you are singing and be repetitive. Watch your baby's reactions, and you'll learn which songs and tunes are his favorites.

9. Read aloud simple rhyming stories—or actually, whatever you enjoy reading for yourself! Your baby will enjoy it all because he is developing his social world with you in it.

Most important, take your cues from your baby. Sometimes your baby (and you!) need downtime. Notice when your baby turns her head away, becomes inattentive, closes or averts her eyes, or becomes fussy or irritated (Murkoff, Eisenberg, and Hathaway 2003, 220–221). This is all about listening to your baby. She is not rejecting you when she turns away; she is communicating with you. *You are interacting, not performing.*

You can also speak to your infant in soothing tones during waking periods and introduce her to guests visiting your house. Take your baby to visit relatives and friends, selecting calm places where your baby won't be alarmed by loud or sudden noises.

Social development can also be stimulated through touch. Play with your baby by encouraging him to hold your finger and giving him a soft back and leg rub to relax. Massage helps your baby learn to control emotions and gives parents and baby a time to bond and connect, according to the Oregon Health and Science University Center for Women's Health. This health center, like many others, recommends massage as a way for parents to learn to read baby's needs and special cues that signal problems or discomfort (https://www.ohsu.edu/womens-health/center-womens-health-birthing-suites).

Don't underestimate the importance of providing socially stimulating experiences for your two-month-old. And social milestones can be some of the most enjoyable—like her first real smile:

https://www.webmd.com/parenting/baby/baby-development-2-month-old#1

https://www.hellomotherhood.com/article/113199-activities-2monthold-infant/

To review other pertinent social developmental leaps, by two months your baby will probably be able to:

- smile to your smile

- respond to a specific sound by startling, crying, or quieting

- may be able to coo and thus vocalize in ways other than crying

- lift his head forty-five degrees on his stomach

- say "Ah-Goo" or similar vowel-consonant combinations

- laugh and squeal as you stimulate him

- recognize the mother in the mirror (https://www.what to expect.com/toddler/self-recognition; Murkoff, Eisenberg, and Hathaway, 2003, 212, 223).

Even though it will be a year or so before you hear your baby's first word, she is already communicating with you constantly. Focus on her bodily behaviors and gestures as well as her sounds and respond to them with encouraging comments. Be a careful observer so that you can catch on to the meanings behind her movements and vocalizations. For example, if your baby wiggles and shivers before her bath, she's telling you that the cold air makes her uncomfortable, so get her in that warm tub quickly. Keeping her covered as much as possible before you lower her into the bath will also help if she doesn't like the feeling of cool air on her naked body.

You can also listen to grunting or coughing sounds. These sounds may mean that she's getting tired, and you'll be able to catch on and settle her down for a nap before fatigue sets in. Notice when your baby stuffs her little fist in her mouth, as she may be telling you that she is waiting to be fed. Through simple observation, you may be able to catch on before she cries—making the beginning of her feeding less difficult. In these ways, as you catch on to her communications, she is feeling your attention and understanding; she knows she matters to you. This is a route to her budding self-esteem that will mature as she grows, because you show her that what she says has meaning in general—and specifically to you!

If you want to understand your baby even better, try and enter her world by squinting your own eyes until everything is a blur. When you then look at someone's face, you will see the contrasts, main forms, and features of their face. You will notice—like your baby does—the black lines on your shirt up against a white background or the dark lines between fingers held together. How wonderful to be able to not only imagine, but actually see what your baby's world is like. (This is what artists do when painting!) Don't forget, in your baby's world, it's your face that your baby likes most of all and uses as a reference to decide what is okay or safe to do next when they are being social, especially when new people are introduced.

Playtime Suggestions

It's all too common for mothers to compare their babies—either to what the baby's own siblings were like at two months old or to other

same-aged babies. Remember, you are simply playing, not witnessing a competition to get into the best preschool or Ivy League
college. Some babies who play less actively speed up in the long run.
So just play at your baby's pace. Here are a few playing tips:

Interactive Play

- Give your baby unconditional love while you play. This
  can be communicated by your calm responses to even
  irritation and fussing.

- Take every opportunity to talk, sing, and coo to your baby
  as you go about your daily routine. *Your goal isn't to teach, but
  to interact and be involved with your infant.*

- Pay more attention to your baby's feedback than what the
  baby books say (including this one). Your baby is unique,
  and his stimulation should be, too. If you relax and enjoy
  your baby, he'll feel loveable. This is your aim.

Helicopter mothers can begin to hover right from the start.
So, give your baby the space he shows you he needs as he averts
his eyes and body when you are overstimulating him. Don't chase
after him, because he'll just dodge your attempts and you won't be
understanding each other.

Independent Play

- Give your baby time to play alone while you keep a
  watchful eye.

- Make sure your baby is in the lead at most playtimes. If
  he is fascinated by the mobile, don't interrupt him with

something else; watch and learn. This builds your baby's self-esteem and sense of agency and initiative.

- Remember that babies have very short attention spans, some shorter than others. If they turn away, they are not rejecting you. They are overstimulated and want to direct the play independently.

Social Play That Builds Self-Esteem

- Toys that help babies with social development include stuffed animals, mobiles, and dolls. Although they can't hug and play with them, they can converse and touch them. Because young infants usually don't grasp objects directly in front of them, offer them from the side.

- It's not too early to praise and cheer when your baby achieves something like reaching for a rattle, lifting his head off the mattress, turning over, or smiling. Do whatever is comfortable to you to reinforce this new learning.

- Notice how your baby reacts to smells or scents in the environment—from when you are cooking, to when he senses the familiar smell of breast or bottle milk—and watch for certain sensitivities unique to your infant. When you are so in tune, your baby knows he matters to you. This builds his self-esteem.

Stimulating Play

- Focus on what stimulates your baby's line of vision rather than what you like to decorate their room with. For example, babies at this stage like bright colors and color contrasts rather than the soft, soothing pastels you may prefer.

- Babies like things that move. Place the mobile on either side of the crib, not overhead, no more than twelve to fifteen inches over the baby's face. Move a rattle or bright toy across the infant's line of vision to encourage the tracking of moving objects. At a pet store, position the baby to watch the fish swim or the birds fluttering in a cage. Blow bubbles for your baby.

- Babies also like stationary objects and spend a lot of time just looking at things. This isn't a waste of time; it's learning time. Geometric patterns or simple faces in black and white are early favorites. Notice that babies are interested in things you might not think of—like the light coming through the blinds.

- Using safe baby mirrors, babies love to glance at themselves—at that other-than-me baby whom they don't recognize! Babies don't usually realize that the baby in the mirror is them until they are between twelve to fifteen months old! (For a test to see if your baby recognizes herself, see the chapter on the twelfth month.)

- Babies like close-up faces, so encourage your friends to say, "hello." Place your baby by another baby and watch their interaction, if there is one.

- Explore the environment; don't stay at home. Babies like to watch everything that moves by them. You don't have to do anything special. Just enjoy your walk in the stroller.

- It is through hearing that babies learn even more. Auditory stimulation is all around—beginning with your voice. In addition to talking and singing, imitate animal sounds and notice how your baby reacts to a cat purring or a dog barking. Crinkle paper and pop a balloon and watch your baby's reaction. Tone it down or tone it up, depending on what you observe. Most important, play back your baby's sounds as they occur. Household sounds are also impressive to a baby, whether it's the blender, the vacuum, a wind chime, or music on your phone.

Play That Builds Sensory Awareness

Have you noticed the specific sounds your baby makes? These interest him the most so imitate them liberally every time you hear one. When you imitate your baby's sounds, he learns how important his sounds are because he attracts your attention. He is learning that his voice is important to you.

- How can you play to capitalize on your baby's fascination with sounds? Find buzzing, squeaking, ringing, and whizzing sounds, and incorporate high-pitched female voices (and don't forget your voices—mother's and father's voices)! With your face close to your baby's, playing is all about having a chat (Rijt, Plooj, and Plas-Plooij 1992, 96). So, coordination between vision and hearing can be stimulating. Don't wait for the baby to reach for the rattle and make a shaking sound, do it for him.

- Play musical toys—especially those that move—to help your baby coordinate sight, sound, and movement. Play

different kinds of music but watch your baby's reactions
so you know when to tone it down.

- Your baby's sense of touch is very important as it is
stimulating and soothing all at once. You send a message
of comfort by the way you bathe, diaper, feed, hold, and
rock your infant. Some babies like to be held firmly, others
loosely. How about yours?

- Most love to be caressed and kissed and have their
tummies tickled lightly or razzed by your lips. You can
blow gently on their fingers and toes. They notice the
differences among those that touch them.

- Notice also their reactions to different textures. Some
babies are very sensitive to somewhat rough materials,
others like the stimulation. Let your baby lie on different
textures, such as the carpet, blanket, or towel, and see how
she responds. Playthings have textures, too, from teddy
bears to wooden blocks, metal bowls, and nubby pillows.

Play That Encourages Motor Development

- Give your baby opportunities for small motor
development with rattles that have handles and can
eventually be passed from hand to hand and mouthed as
well. Though they can't intentionally work activity boards,
they can set off sounds and movements by accident that
are both stimulating and a lot of fun.

- Encourage gross motor development by changing your
baby's position, propping him up into a somewhat

sitting position to have him feel those muscles work, and giving him a new line of vision at the same time. Put him on his tummy and on his back. Place your baby on your shins as you stabilize him with your hands so that he can ride or fly. Motivate rolling over by putting interesting objects on one side of him and then the other. Encourage creeping by having your baby push off against your hands when lying tummy down (Murkoff, Eisenberg, and Hathaway 2003, 244–248).

- Another way to both play and learn more about your baby's preferences is to experiment with bringing objects to her. You will discover how your baby often prefers real things rather than pictures. Move objects, like colorful toys, toward her from various distances, moving them slowly to get her attention. By moving these objects back and forth, close and far, you will discover the distance your baby is interested in. While she can't reach out to grasp something, she can close her little hands around the toy building fine motor coordination. So just put that easy-to-grab object near her busy, waving hands (Rijt, Plooj, and Plas-Plooij 1992, 116–117).

Whatever you do with your two-month-old, remember to play, have fun, and interact. As you and your baby get to know each other with sensory-stimulating experiences, show your enthusiasm often and be aware of when it's time to stop to prevent overstimulation. You know best, because you are getting to know your baby better than anyone!

An Illustration of a Mother and Two-Month-Old Baby at Play

Mommy: "Hi, Sweetie. I see you looking at your mobile. See how it moves. Look at the red and yellow colors. How bright they are."

The mother doesn't interfere with the baby's self-directed play. She just narrates it. She has placed the mobile on the crib's side because she knows babies this age look from left to right rather than straight ahead.

The baby's arms and legs move about excitedly while watching the mobile move. This mobile also has a remote that turns on music. The mother turns it on.

The baby gets even more excited by the sounds she hears. Her eyes widen and her movements become even more frisky.

Mommy: "Whoa! I like the music too. I see your little toes moving and how you open and close your fists. This is so much fun!"

A PLAY SESSION

A sixteen-year-old mother seems deeply ambivalent about being a mother. She sets up the room in an over-stimulating way with about ten toys all around the baby lying on her back. On reflection I realized there was sadness on my part. In general, the baby's mood was low and unengaged and there was a kind of frenzied mood on the mother's part as she anxiously lay more and more toys about. The mother wanting some reaction then puts too many stuffed animals in place of the toys, hoping for a response. But she doesn't engage the baby with the stuffed animals; it's as if she expects the two-month-old to show a desire for them on her own. At some point the mother pointed to one batch of stuffed animals and said they were from the baby's father. She tells me another bunch belonged to her own mother.

The mother's constant talking about herself in a somewhat excited way was an effort to engage with me which she needed but had a disquieting quality because the baby seemed so left out of it. The mother didn't talk to the baby. In fact, at one point she mentioned that she read that babies were supposed to "coo" at this age but hers only "grunted." Then she thought she might be hungry, but I noticed they did not gaze at each other when feeding. It seemed like the baby looked to the side.

I wanted this young mother, who clearly needed maternal care herself, to find that she and the baby could enjoy each other.

"Celia, how about holding your little one in your arms while you sit on this blanket with me. Try showing her just one stuffed animal and make it move up and down."

Celia follows my instructions and says, "Oh, she's watching the monkey. She looks up and down as I move it."

I comment, "Oh, you are playing, and your baby is having fun with you. She likes you when you play with her."

"She likes me? I didn't think so before because she didn't even look at anything I placed around her."

I say, "She needs you to direct her a bit. With too many toys or stuffed animals, she doesn't know where to begin to look. But see how you helped her by showing her just one? Great job!"

"Oh, now she's looking at my face, I think. Maybe she does like me. At least a little."

"Sure. Now try telling her all about the monkey. Even if she doesn't understand your words, she'll like your voice."

"The monkey is brown and soft. 'Hi. Hi, says the monkey.'"

The baby reacts with increased attention and the mother smiles delighted to have affected her baby.

I say, "You and your baby are getting to know each other because you talk to her and notice how much she wants to listen. Your voice is special for her. In fact, it's the most special voice she knows."

"She knows *my* voice? How come?"

"Researchers tell us that babies hear the mommy's voice in utero. So even when you were pregnant, your baby heard your voice. So, when she was born it was the only voice that really mattered, because it was already familiar."

"Really? Now I want to talk more to her. She's making those grunting sounds."

"Let's try and figure out what they mean. She's talking to you."

"Maybe now she is hungry."

"Okay, give it a try. When you give her the bottle, look into her beautiful eyes. Let's see if she looks back."

The young mother holds her baby in her left arm and gives her the bottle with her right hand, a natural position for a mother. She looks in her baby's eyes and they gaze at each other. The baby has become responsive.

"Oh, how she loves looking in your eyes. You both have brown eyes. She looks like you and now you can see, she does like you. You figured out what her grunting was saying. She was talking to you, saying, 'I'm hungry.' But you know, I think she wasn't only hungry for the milk but for you, too. She wants to look at you and have you look at her. I think you're both in good moods now."

"We are! This feels so good."

What Does Celia Learn from Playing with Her Baby?

Most essential to this playtime was that Celia learned she was important to her baby. She didn't have a sense that her baby liked her at first until she played with her effectively, and then the baby, of course, responded with joy. Both this baby's and mother's self-esteem needed boosting.

∽

Like Celia, you and your two-month-old can enjoy not only your baby's growth and development but also playtime that has become even more interactive. This is a wonderful discovery as you find you are enjoying your baby more and more. Now we'll take a look at the third month and see what adventures you will have as your baby grows and matures bit by bit.

Repetition *and* Novelty *with* Your Baby

What Do the Researchers Have to Say about Your Three-Month-Old?

When you hold your three-month-old in your supportive arms, you may be so delighted that you begin to talk in *motherese*, the simplified and repetitive type of speech that uses exaggerated, generally somewhat high-pitched intonation and rhythm. By this age, your baby may respond to your words with coos—followed by *your* coos in response to *hers*.

In this new stage, your baby is able to spontaneously coordinate her expressions, gestures, and voice with your expressions, gestures, and voice, making you remarkably in synch with your baby. It can be a magical age, as you become even more connected to your baby in a very unique way (Gopnik, Meltzoff, and Kuhl 1999).

By three months old, your baby can also detect some cause and effect. For example, infants this age expect that the sound of a voice comes from the same direction as the visually seen location of the face (Stern 1985, 82). They also realize that some of their own actions can influence others' actions.

How do the researchers know this? They observe how babies do and do not understand the relation between actions and results. You can see an example by gently tying one end of a ribbon to your baby's toe and the other end to his mobile making sure there is a little give in the ribbon. When he moves his foot, the mobile moves. He will probably repeat the act, having learned his ability to influence the event. Then, if you give him a chance to do the same thing a week later, he will remember instantly and start kicking.

However, if you disconnect the ribbon, the baby will continue to kick, not realizing the change that occurred. In other words, he makes false assumptions; he doesn't realize that he needs the ribbon's direct connection to the mobile to make it move. Try it and see for yourself. It's so fascinating. You may even notice that your baby coos and smiles as well, as if that will make the mobile move. Oh my, so much to learn!

While smiling and cooing always get a reaction from Daddy, alas, the mobile doesn't respond the same way as Daddy. The mobile does not smile back or move.

This difference between objects and people is something that your three-month-old doesn't understand particularly well just yet. Infants can't discriminate between physical causality with objects, like when baby's foot kicks pull the ribbon and move the mobile, and psychological causality with people, such as when a mother returns a smile or a coo (Gopnik, Meltzoff, and Kuhl

1999, 76). However, they can still detect the source of an action, where it comes from.

Another interesting study to keep in mind as you watch your three-month-old develop is that, according to Stern (1985), a baby at three months old can recognize the difference between self-initiated actions, as when they shake the mobile by kicking their foot, and actions that others initiate.

For example, maternal responses to their babies are much less predictable. For example, a baby can be 100 percent certain that vocalizing will bring a feeling in their chest that resonates. But he can only be fairly certain that when he is making sounds it will result in his mother's vocal response (Messer and Vietze 1982; Stern 1974; Stern 1984, 81). A parent does not walk over and return a coo every single time a baby vocalizes.

In other words, your baby may begin to rely on her own actions more than those of others   as self-initiated actions are the most reliable. However, you can try to be as reliable as possible for her as you respond to her development and growth in encouraging ways.

So, what are some ways you can effectively play with your three-month old?

Infant Development

Movement

Each baby is different, so have fun seeing how your baby develops and grows as you play. Although his arms and legs will still be wobbly, your baby will likely develop some strength in his limbs as you practice sitting, standing, tummy time, and other games. You will also witness your baby's neck strength improving as his head will wobble less and less when you hold him upright. You may even observe that your baby has enough upper-body strength to support his head and chest with his arms while lying on his stomach. He may even have enough lower-body strength to stretch those chubby legs and kick.

As you watch your baby, you should also see some early signs of hand-eye coordination. Your baby's hands may open and shut, come together, swipe at colorful dangling toys, or briefly grab a toy or rattle.

Sleep

There are also important developments occurring when it *isn't* playtime. Your three-month-old's nervous system is maturing, and her stomach is accommodating more milk or formula. These changes should allow your baby to sleep for a stretch of six or seven hours at a time—which means a good night's sleep for you.

If your baby does wake up in the middle of the night, wait about thirty seconds before heading into her room. Sometimes, babies will cry for a few seconds and then go back to sleep. It's important to let your baby rest and learn how to fall back asleep on his own.

When the cries don't stop and you do need to go into your baby's room in the middle of the night, stick to the essentials. Feeding and changing should be done in the dark, if possible. Then put her right back into the crib. Eventually, she will get the idea that nighttime is for sleeping only, not playtime.

Playtime Suggestions

- Respond to your baby's babbling, laughing, and swatting with a lot of smiles and coos in return. (This shows baby you are reliable and predictable.)

- Babies at this age love their hands and feet and can entertain themselves just playing with them. You can extend the play by giving your baby hand and foot rattles; she'll enjoy making sounds for herself. This fosters motor development.

- Gather various toys and other baby-safe household objects and then lie on your stomach in front of your baby—with your face a few feet from his—while he's doing his tummy time. Have him reach for objects. He'll begin to see how his actions cause results.

- For a few minutes, simply walk your fingers up and down and back and forth in front of your baby. Make your fingers dance and skip as if they're trying to catch her. Your baby might just watch happily, or she might reach out to grab your fingers.

- When your baby is in a comfortable position, continue to give him blocks, rattles, soft balls, sturdy vinyl or cloth books, or any baby toys that won't hurt him when he mouths them. Take an item away periodically based on his attentiveness and replace it with something new to explore. Remember, he likes repetition *and* novelty.

- Continue showing your three-month-old items until she is a bit fussy or seems uninterested. At that time, lift her up to face you or sit her up in front of you with support behind her (since she probably won't be able to support her head until she's closer to four months). Then make different faces for her to imitate. You can imitate faces she makes at you as well.

- Play peekaboo with your hands and engage her in conversation. This fosters her learning about objects that aren't seen won't disappear.

- When conversing, *give your baby time to respond*. This will give her a chance to communicate.

- Your baby will enjoy mimicking your sounds. So, make different sounds—remembering to leave gaps in your chatting so that she can react and reply.

- Play music with a strong beat. While it's playing, clap your baby's hands or tap her feet against the floor in rhythm with the music.

- Hold your baby as you dance around the room, singing and humming along with the music and encouraging her to babble along.

- Enjoy carrying your baby around the house, the neighborhood, and the market. Stop every few minutes so that she can explore what's nearby—and don't forget to narrate everything as you go. For example, if you are carrying her around your apartment, say things like, "Look out the window. I see a truck. I see a squirrel."

- Gather some books with pictures to show him one at a time. He may look at the colors or mouth them. Remember cloth and vinyl books are best for baby to play and look at as they like to put everything in their mouth.

- Three-month-old babies enjoy repetition in stories, rhymes, and lullabies. Simply sit quietly with her, listening to her coo along and letting her touch the pages of the book. This is also a wonderful way to help her wind down before a nap.

- Remember to take life slowly with your baby. Don't feel like you have to play with him every minute. He might become overstimulated and fuss, and at other times he might be happy doing nothing but watching you as you cook, use your computer, enjoy a cup of tea, and read to yourself.

- Babies love eggbeaters, spoons, wire whisks, spatulas, books or magazines with pictures, empty bottles of shampoo or conditioner rinsed well with cap removed, colorful fabrics or clothes, fruits, and vegetables. Of course, always supervise your baby as they play with these and other objects or toys.

- Go to your closet! Show your baby your soft sweater, cottony-soft favorite jeans, and brilliantly colored skirt. Run soft or silky fabrics over her face, hands, and feet. You can also lay fuzzy stuff down on the floor and put your baby on top of it.

- Tie or tape some ribbon, fabric, or other interesting streamers onto a wooden spoon and dangle them gently over and in front of your baby's face. Remember, never leave your baby alone with strings or ribbons that could go around his neck or get into his mouth.

- Take a scarf and toss it in the air, letting it settle on your baby's head.

- Tie a toy to an elastic string (like the kind used for cat toys) and bounce it up and down in front of your baby's face, saying "Boing! Boing!" every time it drops away.

- Your baby may like absolutely anything you sing, but "The Wheels on the Bus" is a fun one with movements. (Forgot the words? Make them up or look online.) You can also try adding your baby's name to songs or singing any songs with funny sounds or animal noises in them like "Old McDonald Had a Farm" or "Five Little Ducks."

- Try singing a song in a low growly voice and then in a high squeaky voice to see which gets the best response. Try singing the song breathily into your baby's ear or use a hand puppet to sing to her (a sock works great, too!).

- When you are in the kitchen trying to throw dinner together while your baby is upset, take your baby over to the spice rack and introduce him to the smell of cinnamon. Rub some on your hand and put it up to your baby's nose. (Don't let it get in his eyes or mouth.) If he likes it, try others: vanilla, peppermint, cumin, cloves, or nutmeg. Many other herbs and spices have wonderful aromas that your baby might love—and don't forget about household fragrances like Daddy's shaving lotion or Mommy's hand cream.

- Your baby will enjoy mouthing objects, and you should let her do so—it's part of her exploration and development. Just be careful about what she gets her hands on.

- Get physical if your baby likes it. He may like knee rides or tickle games.

- Blow bubbles on the front porch or in the bathtub when your baby is fussy—or even at the park to attract older kids who will also entertain your baby!

- Run your fingers up and down your baby's belly.

- Add some fun in the tub by aiming a squirt bottle at your baby's toes.

- When you find that your baby can hold her head up securely, hoist her into the air. Play like she's a rocket ship, flying her over you and making realistic rocket noises. Make believe that your baby is an elevator, advancing up floor by floor and then down again, until you say, "Boo! You've made the trip!"

- A baby-safe unbreakable mirror can be fun for the three-month-old as well as a winning way to spend tummy time, which is otherwise something small babies often don't like. Just place the mirror in front of your baby's face so that he has to use his neck muscles to look at himself.

- Any easy-to-grab, lightweight rattles, rings, and stuffed animals are a good idea.

- If your baby is able to lift her neck, then she may like being pulled by her little arms from an almost sitting to standing position.

What else should you keep in mind? Babies who are on the quiet side need your participation more than ever, so give them a bit more encouragement with your stimulation. If you catch on to a leap in development, grab the moment. That's when your baby is really eager to learn.

Also, don't forget to give your baby independent play—especially by ten weeks. This will allow you to both get a small break and encourage development. Simply put your baby on their back on a play cloth and watch him reach for hanging toys, swipe at them, or even swing them back and forth—amusing himself on his own (Rijt, Plooj, and Plas-Plooij 1992, 119).

How exciting that your three-month-old's sensory awareness is growing by leaps and bounds, as is your relationship with her! Stay in synch with *novelty* and *repetition*. She loves whatever you do and say and will watch intently and coo in response—also remember to take breaks whenever downtime is needed for both of you.

An Illustration of a Mother and Three-Month-Old Baby at Play

Mommy: "Sweetie, we're going to have some fun. I can help you fly. (Lift baby.) Oh, my. You're like a rocket. Whoo! There you go flying."

The baby smiles and giggles and wants you to do it again.

You repeat this action several times.

Mommy: "Oh, listen to you laugh! I'm laughing too. This is fun for both of us."

A PLAY SESSION

Let me tell you all about how sixteen-year-old Liv played with me with her three-month-old baby in infant-parent psychotherapy.

She chats to him smiling and he gazes at her and smiles back making little quiet sounds. I tell her about how researchers around the world think being a mother like her is so important that they have studied mothers and babies. I play with her baby just by talking in *motherese* and he responds more actively, cooing loudly.

Dr. Hollman: "Liv, you look excited."

Liv: "He was so much louder with you. Why did you talk in that funny way instead of your usual voice with me?"

Dr. Hollman: "How great you noticed that. You can do it, too. It's called *motherese*, which just means to talk in a high sing-song kind of way. Babies love that more than grown-up talk like you and I do. Do you want to try it?"

Liv immediately says in a higher, singing type voice, "Hello my baby. Coo for me so much like with Dr. Hollman. Aren't you cute putting your tongue out."

The baby coos with excitement picking up Liv's enthusiasm. They stick out tongues to each other. Liv is laughing and the baby smiles broadly, imitating her.

What Does Liv Discover
When Playing with Her Baby?

It's wonderful to see how pleased both Liv and her baby are with this simple use of what she learned from research such as the use of *motherese*! Liv is quite proud to know she used research about babies, and it worked like magic!

$\sim$

How delightful it is to learn about research, development, and play with your three-month-old. Not only does your baby learn a lot, but as parents you do, too!

The Impact of Communicating with Your Baby

What Do Researchers Have to Say about Your Four-Month-Old?

How mothers and four-month-old infants interact indicates the kind of play they can have together. Parenting practices such as responsiveness, devotion, investment, and involvement are important for mother and baby. In 2016, Dr. Beatrice Beebe and her colleagues studied videos of mothers with their four-month-olds to determine the impact that their communications have on their attachment styles at one year. In the study, you can see how each partner affects the other from one moment to the next. As you may have discovered, four-month-olds are very communicative—especially with their caregivers.

[Babies] perceive and respond to every little shift in the parent's facial and vocal emotion, touch quality, and orientation. . . . Based on the extent to which the infant uses the parent as a secure base from which to explore, and as a safe haven when distressed, infants can be classified as having secure or insecure attachment patterns. (Beebe, Cohen, and Lachmannn 2016, 2)

It is amazing to see how much was learned from simple observation of face-to-face interactions between babies and their mothers. Beebe studied four-month-old babies and then followed the same baby and mother pairs up to the babies' first year. Mothers and babies were videoed as they interacted. This was shown on one screen. Then another screen was used which split the frontal view of the mother placed next to the frontal view of the baby.

In this way, the viewer could observe each partner's actions and reactions from both perspectives in split seconds. These interactions set "the trajectory for patterns of relatedness and intimacy over the [baby's] lifetime" (2). Researchers were able to look at the quality of a mother and baby's interactions and then predict whether their attachment (connections based on these interactions) would be termed secure or insecure when the baby reached twelve months. It is outstanding what a mother and baby can communicate through simple and quick facial and vocal expressions—some moments of interaction lasted only one third of a second (5)!

When we reach twelve months, we'll be able to identify secure and insecure attachments. For now, enjoy the new interactions you are having with your baby.

The Action-Dialogue World

Infants and mothers live in a "split-second world" during face-to-face interaction (Stern 1985; Beebe, Cohen, and Lachmannn 2016, 41). For play to be effective, the two partners in time become predictable and anticipate each other's moves.

But how do we know that four-month-olds can anticipate events? In an experiment by Haith, Hazen, and Goodman (1988), infants aged three and a half months saw two series of slides of checkerboards, bull's-eyes, and drawings of faces. One series was predictable; it alternated to the left and to the right in a steady rhythm as the images moved up and down. The other series was random in left or right positions; the infants could not detect a pattern. The researchers videotaped one of the infant's eyes and found that the infants were able to recognize the pattern of the regularly alternating series and even showed anticipatory eye movements. "Their eyes focused on the slide a fraction of a second before it appeared. This ability to detect sequences of actions, to generate expectancies, and to anticipate events gives the infant a way of maintaining continuity in an ever-changing world" (Beebe, Cohen, and Lachmann 2016, 41). Thus, infants at this age are able to learn "As *I* do this, then *I* do that," "As *you* do this, then *you* do that" (41).

Understanding this action-dialogue helps us see that infants come to expect the following scenarios:

- "As I look at you (mother) and begin to smile, I open my mouth and raise my head more and more until I am bursting with my biggest smile."

- "Mother, as your smile widens, your mouth opens more, and your head goes up and up."

- "As I open my mouth in bigger and bigger smiles, you (mother) smile at me and open your mouth and raise your head up until we are both reaching our smiles up and up toward each other."

- "As you (mother) open your mouth and smile at me, I return your smile and open my own mouth more and more." (41–42)

These sequences are learned by your baby as action sequences and don't require verbal language; in fact, most are learned through simple conscious awareness. As the sequences are repeated, your baby comes to expect, anticipate, and remember them. This is the action-dialogue language that guides your infant in her relationship with you.

All of this supports the earlier stated truth that infants and babies love repetition but also novelty. As you play with your baby and watch him grow, he will thrive on both repetition and variety. Try new things, but also allow your baby to anticipate events by getting used to his environment and enjoying what he already knows.

Infant Development

Coordinating Communication

While your infant showed facial expressions prior to birth, from two to four months his expressions become fully communicative and animated. At this point in your baby's development, face-to-face interaction sets patterns of relatedness and intimacy that will grow over his life span—revealing communication abilities that will grow and grow!

There is a vocal rhythm between mother and baby that is coordinated during their face-to-face play. These interactions at four months predict the interactions at twelve months. It is as if the mother is an *amplifying mirror* of her baby. The baby sees herself resonating in the mother's eyes. This resonance is called *intersubjective* because the baby and parent cannot be seen as separate from each other but must be considered to be mutually influencing each other through *intersubjective resonance* that is created by both or co-created (Ammaniti and Trentini 2009, 545).

As mother and baby interact and play, their minds or intents affect each other continuously. You can think of this as a song being sung by a choir, only the choir is made of mother and baby. Together their voices, or smiles, coos, and actions, affect each other and blend and resonate, creating together (or what is termed *co-creating*) their connection.

However, as babies and mothers play, they are not always in concert. Emotions are reflected in the eyes, facial expressions, head orientations, and hands of the mother and her infant, and there are often times when mother and baby are out of sync. This is normal and expected.

Mismatch in Communication

It is important to understand that when mothers and babies communicate and interact there is periodically a rupture or mismatch in how they are relating. The reparation or remedying of this occurs often, so you needn't worry about always communicating right on target. The baby may be looking out the window at the

light coming in through the blinds and the mother may be seeking her baby's attention on her at the same moment. This is a
mismatch, but soon mothers learn that light draws their baby's
attention, and they can join in this delightful experience their
baby is having by saying something like, "Ooh. Look at all that
light coming in from the blinds. How beautiful, sweetie." Then
the infant will naturally turn to the mother's voice, and she will
receive the attention she seeks and, in effect, repair the mismatch
naturally and easily.

"During these moments of mismatch, the infant is able to
propose several motor and expressive schemes (such as crying,
protest, or funny faces) to re-establish a level of contingency with
the mother" (Ammaniti and Trentini 2009, 547). Contingency
learning refers to the relationship between a baby's actions and
behavior, and what happens in response. The response is *contingent*
on the baby's behavior. Sensitive mothers attune to their infant's
emotions and respond to their initiatives to interact. This strongly
suggests that the mother-infant communication seen in play is
helpful for a baby's development.

There is an early process in mother-infant communication
seen in play. By four to six months, patterns of interaction are
becoming predictable. As a parent, you will communicate with
your baby mostly through attention (gazing at and away from
the baby's face), emotion (positive to negative infant and mother
facial and vocal expressions), orientation (sitting upright, leaning
forward, or looming in, and the infant's head facing toward the
mother or arching away), gaze, facial expression, and touch.

Luckily, by four to six months, your patterns of interaction with
your baby are becoming much more organized and predictable,
allowing you to be sensitive when there are moments of mismatch.

Eye Love

During play, special communication moments can occur, such as *eye love*, when mothers and infants sustain a mutual gaze for up to 100 seconds with positive affect (Ammaniti and Trentini 2009, 22).

This parent-infant process cannot be explained based on either partner alone. The parent and infant co-create the nature of the infant's experience (Beebe, Cohen, and Lachmannn 2016, 13). In other words, mommy and baby work together interacting when they play. Interestingly, a mother tends to look at her baby's face most of the time, while the infant is the one who makes and breaks the mutual gaze—looking away and looking back in order to regulate arousal. (This is also a time when your communication might misalign or be out of synch, as your baby may need to dampen or lessen her arousal when you want to stimulate her with eye contact.)

How Do Infants and Parents Sense the State of the Other?

Infants and their mothers sense each other by reading how the other responds to different behaviors. For example, a mother can sense her baby's state by talking to and imitating her baby during playtime. If the mother matches her baby's sounds well, the baby feels that "someone is on his wave-length" (Beebe, Cohen, and Lachmann 2016, 31). This creates rapport. When a mother can share a "woe" face (33) in response to her baby's distress, there is a rapport—similar to when positive interactions occur.

However, rapport is not always the outcome here. As mentioned above, mismatching can occur. If the mother and infant continue to overly escalate the arousal of the other, the baby may become so distressed that she vomits. If this is typical for a mother and her baby, the result will be a severely insecure attachment—without rapport—by twelve months.

To avoid such mutual escalation, a mother needs to regain or learn, maybe for the first time, perhaps from another caretaker, how to be sensitively attuned to her baby's comfort level of arousal when interacting. It's not as difficult as this may seem. If you see your baby avert her head over and over, turning farther and farther away from the front of your face, you will soon catch on that she is over aroused and trying to tell you that without words. Simply follow your baby's lead and everything will be fine.

An additional way parents sense the mental state of their infant is through *mirror neurons*. This occurs when the mother understands the baby's intention by understanding what her own intention would be if she were doing the same thing. Due to this social interaction, emotions are communicated in play. For example, if a mother sees her baby reach out with her little fingers, she is most likely wanting to touch the mother's hand. It's so natural for a mother to almost instinctively feel this and she will respond by giving the baby her hand to play with.

Another source is called *embodied simulation*, or when the action of either baby or mother influences the other's *perception* of their partner's action. This is most effective when the mother or baby is in tune with the subtle nuances of her partner's emotions and expressions—such as her gestures and postures (Beebe, Cohen, and Lachmann 2016, 34). Let's say the baby leans forward when she is sitting on your lap facing outward. If you look and see what she is seeing, you'll know what is influencing her. Holding on to her for safety, let her reach out to the object or person she is seeking, and she'll be delighted that you perceived what she intended. As her hand makes contact with the object or person, she's enchanted with you, and she will feel in concert.

On the other hand, when the baby is on the mother's lap facing the mother's face and the mother sticks out her tongue, the baby will most likely imitate her or at least open her mouth widely. The baby's action shows the baby understands what the mother did.

Again, when the baby does what the mother just did, the baby is more able to understand it. This is especially the case when the baby imitates the gestures and postures of the parent.

The Optimal Midrange Model

When playing with your four-month-old, more is not necessarily better. *Midrange coordination* is preferable and provides the most secure and flexible attachment. Midrange coordination refers to the combination of vocal rhythms and gestures that a mother and her baby use to stay in tune with each other. This means that the two are coordinating their sounds *and* their silences; that is, altering their behavior, based on what the other just did (Beebe, Cohen, and Lachmann 2016, 35).

As a mother shortens and elongates the duration of her sounds with her baby, different levels of coordination can be seen. Studies have shown that a midrange or medium level of coordination predicts the most secure level of attachment at twelve months. If the coordination between mother and baby is very high or very low, it predicts an insecure attachment at twelve months.

In other words, it is important for the mother to *coordinate* her sounds to her baby's (as well as she can) rather than trying to exactly *imitate* her baby's sounds. This usually happens naturally. That is, when mothers approximately match their babies sounds, they are creating midrange interactions. These four-month-olds feel that their mothers are in synch with them.

How do you avoid coordination that is too high or low? High coordination is when the mother tries too hard and is vigilant. On the flip side, low coordination means that there is a withdrawal; both mother and baby are behaving relatively independently of the other and neither is adjusting to the other's behavior. Slowing down, sitting back, and waiting to see what your four-month-old does next can allow both you and your baby time to readjust to each other. When playing, you will know your baby is distressed when you see expressions such as a grimace, frown, compressed lips, fussing, whimpering, or even angry protests and crying.

When your baby is distressed during play, there are things you can do to calm him without "trying too hard." For example, you can loosely, empathically join or match your infant's fuss or cry rhythm with your own empathic vocal woe voice and face. The distress is approximately matched, but not the volume or intensity—which would risk overstimulating the baby. When you subtly match your infant's distress in a quiet and soothing way, the baby knows that he is sensed and feels better. Once the baby has been joined in this way, he can continue to regulate his distress. Then, both mother and baby can gradually calm down (Beebe, Cohen, and Lachmann 2016; Gergely and Watson 1996; Stern 1985).

If your baby can continue to look at you during her distress, de-escalation or ramping down of her distress occurs most easily. So, babies actually shape their mother's responses. They contribute "to the cocreation of distress regulation" (Beebe 2000; Beebe, Cohen, and Lachmann 2016, 36). Isn't it amazing that your baby can help you know how to calm her down and that the two of you work together to return to a relaxed and contented state?

You needn't worry about being absolutely in tune with your infant. When there is a rupture in the interaction, it can easily be repaired by an empathic mother. In fact, this is very natural and common. Such *mismatched states* or *interactive errors* happen "approximately two thirds of the time in face-to-face interactions" (Beebe, Cohen, and Lachmann 2016, 37). Remarkably, transitions back and forth occur once every three to five seconds. They are a part of normal interactive play and mother-baby conversations. It's not unusual for a mother to intuit that her baby isn't reacting happily, so slow down for a moment in time, and wait for your infant to rejoin you.

Here is a slow, video-like example of disruption and repair of play: The infant turns slightly away and arches her back while the mother is smiling slightly. The infant's eyes are closed briefly, and her bottom lip is drawn in. The mother also pulls in her bottom lip, matching this infant expression as if to say, "uh-oh." She senses her baby's state. This moment may last one second and is barely perceptible to an onlooker. Then the infant reaches for her mother, and the mother reaches for her baby's hands. The rupture has been repaired, and they continue playing as if nothing has happened (Beebe, Cohen, and Lachmann 2016).

During play the baby has a *say*—that is, the power of refusal—by turning away. But the mother still may continue to chase the baby, failing to respond to the baby's cues. The baby can simply continue to turn away until his mother catches on. Sometimes, however, the mother doesn't catch on. So, the baby increases her protest. At worst, the baby may protest vocally, arch her back, go limp, or freeze. This is called an aversive interaction referred to as "chase and dodge" (39). The mother chases; the baby dodges.

Again, this can be easily avoided by being observant of your baby's behavior and not pursuing him (chasing him) when he turns away (dodging) showing moments of distress. In pursuing a baby that wants her space, you may be overreacting and not seeing what your baby really needs. Her reactions tip you off so you can change your momentum.

Playtime Suggestions

Now that we've discussed the exciting developments that your baby is experiencing at four months old, what are some good ways to encourage her development through play?

A simple place to start is playing peekaboo. It requires no toys whatsoever and is very apropos for this age, when your baby is learning how you appear, disappear, and reappear. This game teaches *object permanence*: when an object isn't seen, it still exists. Stuffed animals are very enjoyable at this age as well—keeping in mind a few safety tips:

- Eyes or noses on stuffed animals must not be small objects like buttons, because they may be a choking hazard.

- No wires should be used to attach parts—even if covered by fabric—in case chewing or wearing off presents a hazard of a puncture.

- Don't attach a string longer than six inches to the stuffed animal.

- Check seams so that stuffing won't come out (a choking hazard).

- Make sure stuffed animals are washable so they don't collect germs.

- Don't put stuffed animals in your baby's crib, because this could result in suffocation. (Murkoff, Eisenberg, and Hathaway 2003, 308)

Toys that are stimulating to the senses are perfect for four-month-olds. Some great ideas are: a mirror or mobile (sight), a clown with a chime (sound), a cradle gym or activity board (touch), or a teething ring (taste). When you're sure that your baby's toys are safe, there are so many possibilities including all kinds of rattles that make different sounds; hitting a rubber spoon on a drum; and holding up picture books, turning each page and naming objects.

Keep in mind that four-month-old babies are very social and responsive, so capitalize on your baby's intense desire to interact with you and take time to *play*. Of course, remain keenly aware of when she is over- or understimulated. Finally, remember that despite all of this research data, your baby is not a research subject. She is a loved one who enjoys you delighting in her! This is communication at its best.

An Illustration of a Mother and Four-Month-Old Baby at Play

Mommy and baby are facing each other while the baby is propped up to sit against many pillows on the couch.

Mommy: "Hey. Wa-a-tch carefully! See this blanket? (Mother covers her face with the small blanket.) Where is Mommy?"

The baby stares and waits a few seconds until the mother dramatically says, "Swoosh. Off it comes."

The baby giggles and laughs. The mother repeats this play three times, each time getting escalating laughter. Daddy is watching, too, also enjoying these delightful moments.

Then the mother puts the blanket gently on the baby's face.

"Ooh. Where did you go?"

The mother removes the blanket and sees the baby's eyes open wide and grin.

The mother does it several times each time getting an escalating giggle.

A PLAY SESSION

Sometimes when I visit a mother in her home there are family members there and I can observe their interactions with each other with the baby cluing me in at the same time to how the mother is feeling about mothering her baby in mixed company.

Here is a description of such a visit.

I climb on wooden steps to knock on the door. I am let in by twenty-two-year-old Caz who introduces me to her mother and brother, Ward, who are there cleaning out the apartment.

The grandmother says, "I hope it's okay that we're here."

I say, "It's fine. Looks like you have a lot to do."

The grandmother is a round-faced woman in her forties. She is friendly enough but not at all concerned with finding me a place to sit. Caz isn't concerned where I should go either.

I can see the full range of the apartment now. There are two bedrooms and a living room connected to a small kitchen. I ask if I could move a chair to which Caz says, "Of course," and I put it by the baby who is on the side of the living room sleeping contentedly in a swing with some music on.

The grandmother seems in charge of the baby while Caz and her brother are arranging and moving things around. Because the baby is sleeping, they are attending to the apartment, and Caz's mother tells me,

"We believe in talking and doing whatever might make noise while the baby sleeps."

Ward says, "We have an aunt who makes everyone be silent while the baby sleeps."

Caz says, "We're not like that."

Ward tells me. "Caz taught Semantha how to stick her tongue out."

I ask Caz, "How'd you do that?"

"I stuck my tongue out, and she did, too. It was simple."

I add, "It was simple because your baby has learned to imitate you. She is watching your face closely, because you're so important to her and doing what you do."

Eventually the baby, Semantha, awakens, and she looks like her eyes are fixed on mine, but actually I think she is fixed on the light coming from an open window.

The grandmother is attentive to the baby. She comes over and talks to her, "Oh how beautiful and smart you are!" The baby responds with a smile and efforts to speak, babbling a bit.

I find myself enjoying the baby more than ever before and being conscious of initiating talk with Caz, lest she feel left out of my attention. But Caz seems quite content with me sitting by the baby while she works around the apartment. A few times the grandmother chastises the brother to help Caz more.

The baby goes back to sleep in her cute pink onesie. I seem to be the first to notice when she is waking up again and babbling a bit, but the grandmother catches on quickly, too, noting her arousal and goes to get her out of the seat.

Caz goes to microwave the bottle. There is some talk between the grandmother and Caz about if the milk is good.

Caz says, "It's from last night and it is." After it is heated the grandmother thinks it might be too hot.

Caz says the bottle is hot, but the milk is only warm. The grandmother feeds her holding her lovingly. The grandmother seems more confident at mothering than Caz.

Caz says to me, "She is sleeping more during the day than at night. So, she was up all night every two hours."

Caz explains, "We all slept at my mother's house because of Yom Kippur."

I ask, "How many ounces does Semantha drink?"

"It is a four-ounce bottle."

Although Semantha takes about two breaks from feeding, she seems to finish it.

Caz says, "She's smiling more now. Look at her tongue move between her lips."

I comment, "How observant you are."

Caz responds, "She weighs nine pounds and I think, well my mother thinks, I overfeed her."

I say, "I guess since your mother is so experienced, it's hard to decide on your point of view, too."

She looks at me curiously obviously hearing my comment and considering it quietly.

After the baby is finished being fed by the grandmother, she is put back in the swing. Then Ward was assigned the task of watching the baby. Ward mimics his mother's high voice when she talked to the baby. This is an indication to me that the grandmother knows how to talk to a baby and elicit her attention. Then he talks in an even higher voice and the baby responds with a smile and a coo. He is pleased.

I ask Caz, "Is Semantha going to day care today?"

Caz says, "No, tomorrow, and I'll have a panic attack. I'm scared."

"What are you scared about?" I gently ask.

"I'm used to being with her twenty-four seven. I'm afraid the baby won't like me anymore."

"I understand your worry, but by now Semantha knows your face and your voice, and she won't forget it."

Caz smiles in relief. She says, "Look how she holds her head up without anyone holding it."

"I see that. You are becoming a really great observer. Is she ever put on her stomach to see if she holds her head up then?"

Caz says, "When I do that (lay her on her stomach) she cries."

She tries anyway and Semantha doesn't cry and tries a bit to lift her head.

"Look at her! Great, Caz, for trying. She's not as fragile as you think. Up went her head. The more you try, the stronger she'll get," I say.

I comment to Caz, "So again, you know what Semantha is saying just by the look on her face. You knew from her expression, as you said, when she is going to the bathroom. You are getting to know her so well."

"Oh. I guess you're saying that so I can be glad about that."

"Yes. Absolutely. Knowing what her expressions mean is all about being the good mother you're trying so hard to be."

It is time to go, and I tell Caz it was a fun visit.

"Semantha's getting so strong. I'm glad you try things and aren't afraid when she cries. Also, don't forget, she'll watch you carefully when you pick her up at day care. Next week, you can tell me how it goes."

Caz says, "I will. See you next week?"

I say, "Of course, every week. It was nice to meet you all."

What Does Caz Learn Playing with Semantha?

Though this family worked well as a unit and between the three of them the baby got enough positive attention, the least attentive was Caz. Yet, I think by the end of the hour, she heard me clearly suggesting she could mother Semantha just like her mother and that she didn't have to be afraid if Semantha cried, and so Caz tried tummy time again with great success. She also learned to be less afraid of leaving Semantha at day care, a natural concern, because I reminded her that she would be recognized again by her face and voice. It was as if Caz was uncertain that she had her own specific relationship with Semantha, even calling her "the baby" rather than using her name.

It was clearly important for Caz to hear me treating her as the mother, rather than the grandmother, and to boost her confidence as a mother, because the grandmother kept taking charge when they were all together. I wanted Caz to consider that she had thoughts of her own, encouraging her implicitly to speak up for herself.

~

You, too, may experience others trying to take over for you as you mother your baby. It's okay to be the one in charge even if you are experimenting by trial and error what works well with your baby. Your confidence will build as you interact more and more.

Exploring and Discovering with Your Baby

What Do Researchers Have to Say about Your Five-Month-Old?

Your baby is now doing more than looking at the world and mouthing it, she is touching it, too. She is discovering and exploring whatever is in reach with her little hands and, of course, with her little mouth, too.

Babies are discriminating between sounds. We can't ask babies directly whether they think two sounds are the same, but we can find out through simple experiments. In one such experiment, newborn babies tell us what they hear by sucking on a special nipple that is connected to a computer. There is one loud sound played from a speaker for each hard suck. Babies in the study sucked up to eighty times a minute to keep the sound turning on until they got bored and their sucking would slow—only to speed up again when a new sound was introduced. The change in their sucking shows that babies know the differences between new and old sounds.

Clearly even young babies know more about language than we may have imagined, so keep on talking and singing to them! By four months this sucking experiment loses its zing, but as five to six months roll around another test works as well. When different sounds come from a loudspeaker and a black box lights up with a bear or monkey moving on it, the baby turns. Soon the babies figure out to turn their heads toward the loudspeaker when the sound changes, letting us know that they heard the sound difference. Five-month-olds can barely distinguish this change but wait until next month!

Infant Development

According to Murkoff, Eisenberg, and Hathaway (2003, 310–311), when deciding how you want to play with your five-month-old, you should keep in mind what he can already do developmentally:

- when upright, holds head steady

- lies on her tummy, raising her chest with her arms

- continues to pay attention to small objects

- reaches for and grasps objects

- squeals and smiles—especially when you smile at her

- keeps her head level with her body if pulled into a sitting position

- rolls over (one way or both ways)

- bears some weight on her legs and even stands while holding on to someone or something

- turns toward voices

- sits with support

- pulls up to a standing position from sitting

- works to get a toy that is out of reach, objecting if you try and take it away

- passes objects from one hand to the other

- looks for lost objects

- babbles with vowel and consonant combos such as ga-ga-ga, ba-ba-ba, ma-ma-ma, and da-da-da

This list can give you a great starting point in realizing what your baby is already capable of doing, what she enjoys doing, and what kind of play might interest her most. Your child may or may not be doing all of these things—remember, developmental milestones vary greatly from baby to baby!

Movement

Once your baby can make several smooth movements in a sequence, you will notice that she will take even more opportunities to grab objects in her reach. You might even see her shake playthings side to side or up and down, or press, push, or shake a toy over and over. This means that your baby can now make her movements flow into each other. For example, she may grab an object with one hand and then pass it to her mouth. Watch your baby correct her movements as she practices this flow, grabbing and picking things up. You may notice that she has developed preferences (Rijt, Plooj, and Plas-Plooij 1992, 169)!

Separation Anxiety

Your baby may be beginning to show signs of separation anxiety as his object permanence improves. Signs of separation anxiety are when your baby fusses or cries when you are parting because he is not yet able to know when you leave that you'll return. Even though your baby may be aware that when an object is removed, it can be found again, it takes up to three years for the baby to be fully aware this is also true with people, which we call object constancy.

Try to say words like "hello" and "bye-bye" to him, watching his reactions when you appear and disappear. This is just the beginning of helping him with understanding that will grow over time. First, however, he learns what disappears will reappear with toys or objects so begin there. Cover a toy and say, "Where did it go?" and then make it appear, saying, "Oh. Here it is again." Your baby will love this game because it's just what he's trying to master.

Language

What is new about your baby's language development that you can incorporate into your play? At this point babies seem to think all sounds are rapid talk. There is a mysterious gap between the sound waves that reach your baby's ears and the sound combos she creates in her mind—learning language is a complicated business! Even simple sounds like "ah" are said differently depending on who says them. And when we speak more quickly or slowly, the sound waves change all the time. Further, each time a consonant is put in front of a different vowel, the sound changes. Your baby isn't a computer with a coding program, yet that is what she is faced with as she picks up the sounds you make. Your child cannot actually understand the differences between the way mommy and daddy say the same words until she is about three years old. But babies know important things about language from birth and learn a great deal more before they say their first word.

Most of what your five-month-old is learning is the sound system of language. If she says a sound that approaches a word like "da-da," daddy will respond, imitate it, and reinforce it with a big smile. With this positive reinforcement, you'll hear the sound more often—even though your baby doesn't know what it means. Your baby will try to imitate your inflections of his sounds. Try some variations and see your baby's surprise as she hears the difference. The effort she puts into this may tire her out, but, rest assured, she is learning. Alternatively, your baby may also interrupt grown-up conversations with her vocalizing, trying to bring back more attention to her! So, accede to her wishes and make her the focus.

Quieter babies also experiment with new little noises, but they may not always be happy to hear new sounds, so be careful. Introducing too many new sounds may shut her down. Your baby may want to experiment on her own, expanding her sense of agency and demonstrating volition. This is in accord with Stern's (1985) theory that a baby develops an organized sense of a core self from two to seven months. Your five-month-old is generally on this timetable, and it is affecting her growing language development.

Bonding with Mother

By five months old, a baby can ordinarily recognize his mother—with all her subtleties. Experiences have produced memories of her caretaking, and when disturbing experiences occur, the baby knows that mother will minister to him and make him feel better. Such relief becomes "confidently expected" (Mahler, Pine, and Bergman 1975). Babies with this healthy relationship develop a *preferential smiling response* to their mother; this is a crucial sign that the baby has memory of his mother helping him.

So, when you play with a baby and he seems distressed, you can relieve the distress with careful attunement to what went awry. By five months, that specific bond between baby and mother is more and more established.

Playtime Suggestions

One of the first things to keep in mind while playing with your five-month-old is to continue with a lot of face-to-face interaction. And by all means, don't forget everything you've already learned about communicating with your baby! Here are some ideas for play—some only slightly changed to please your slightly older baby.

- Your five-month-old will love hearing different sounds, seeing funny faces, and singing and dancing to a strong beat.

- Rev her up by visiting other babies when going to a playground.

- Swings with a high back are exciting for a baby this age, if you don't push too hard.

- Increase your skin contact, cuddling with your tops taken off.

- Since babies love to splash in water, bathe your baby for fun and for play, and start attending baby swim classes if you like.

- An unbreakable baby-safe mirror is a lot of fun, as it allows your little one to talk with "another" baby!

- Find balls and toys that make little noises, as they are very exciting to your sound-making cherub.

- Place baby on her tummy with a roly-poly toy within her reach. It will right itself as she bats it or as you playfully wobble it for her (Open Hands Media AB).

- Play peekaboo and observe how your baby's focus will shift to the "boo!" This is teaching your baby object permanence (an object that is moved out of sight hasn't disappeared).

- Put colorful objects in front of your baby and move them back and forth, as she can now discern tiny items with a lot of color and can track moving objects.

- As your baby passes one object from hand to hand, interfere and take your turn, too. Interacting this way is playing.

- Put your baby in a bounce chair or a swing, which can keep her entertained for hours! Don't forget to visit with her at the same time.

- With the increase in attention span that older babies develop, your baby may lie on her back or sit in her chair playing for an hour and a half to two hours happily.

- Let your baby touch, hold, turn, and examine her toys. Her eyes, fingers, and mouth will now be integrated as she learns.

- Rolling over can be a fun game for your baby to play once she figures out how.

- Your baby is babbling more than ever, so take advantage of opportunities to talk with her. Narrate what you're doing with her as you bathe, diaper, and sing to her in the bathtub.

- Since your baby's hearing and vision are almost completely developed, notice that *your baby might understand her name.* Whisper and sing her name to her and see if she turns to you when you spontaneously call her (What to Expect 2018).

- If your baby doesn't babble, don't worry. Quieter babies also progress and play as they suck on fingers and toys with increasing intensity and bring their feet to their mouths to suck on their toes.

- Your baby will love to mouth and chew on every edge of a toy, enjoying each separate part.

  - Babies may even wave their hands as they hold on to things—each hand imitating the other. Next, try waving objects yourself to see if your baby imitates you.

It's been an exciting five months with your baby, and she is now in better touch with her language, movement, and interactions with others. This is a lively time in your child's development— and it will only increase in the sixth month. Two to six months is a highly social time of life, during which your five-month-old is learning rapidly and engaging with you personally. As every month brings new excitements, discovery, and fun, don't forget to *play* with your baby!

An Illustration of a Mother and Five-Month-Old Baby at Play

A mother who enjoys sound play sets up a big cloth for her baby to lie on tummy down and introduces each new toy to see her baby's reaction.

Mommy: "Listen to the sound of this big red rattle."

She shakes it and it makes a clacking sound and then the baby takes it and shakes it, too, and smiles. When the mother introduces a second rattle with a squeaking sound, she reaches to remove the first rattle from her baby's hand. The baby makes little crying sounds. She doesn't want to give it up.

The mother catches on and puts the second rattle in her baby's other hand. With her little grip, she squeaks it by accident. Then she does it on purpose over and over and drops the first rattle now that her attention has been shifted.

Mommy is delighted.

"You love different sounds. Let's try some more."

Mommy takes some wrapping paper and crinkles it loudly in front of the baby who is now sitting up.

The baby grabs it and crinkles it, too, giggling at the sound she's making all on her own.

Mommy is so pleased, she grabs her iPhone to snap a picture as the baby crinkles the paper, but when the baby hears the clicking of the phone, she shifts her attention once more.

This mother is so pleased that her baby recognizes and is curious about all different sounds. This is really fun play that will eventually increase language development because new sounds have become so interesting.

A PLAY SESSION

Twenty-two-year-old Caz and I had not seen one another for approximately a month. When I look at

Semantha whom she is carrying in her arm, I spontaneously comment how even more beautiful she has become. Caz takes us into the kitchen where she had prepared oatmeal in one bowl and bananas in another. I comment, "and she has begun eating food and saying many more baby sounds."

Caz shows me the special spoons that Mark (new boyfriend) had bought her that turned different colors depending on how hot the food was to protect the baby from something too hot. Caz tastes the food on the spoon first though before she gives it to the baby. Caz tells me that Semantha likes oatmeal, but tonight is the first time with bananas. She says, "Every three days I try a new food."

Caz plays with Semantha as she feeds her, tapping her little toes that Semantha has become enchanted with friskily moving them and grabbing for them. Caz kisses her several times and taps her tummy saying, "Yummy, yummy." Semantha revels in this attention and smiles and speaks her new sounds that have a high pitch. Caz says, "She makes ma-ma and da-da sounds but has no idea what she is saying."

The feeding is going so well that it is surprising that Semantha starts to complain and manages to put her thumb in her mouth for a bit. Caz waits patiently. When the thumb comes out the food goes in. But Semantha still complains, not crying at all but making complaining sounds of ah (like in bat) "ah ah ah," and Caz just waits it out telling her it is time to eat before the bottle, and she has to eat so Mommy can sleep tonight. This is said in a merry kind of way. How lovely it is to see them have a conversation. I comment. "When you're so patient with her eating, Semantha becomes patient too, a very nice accomplishment."

It seems that Caz had learned a lot herself in the month I didn't see her. She is so very much more in tune and responsive.

In the midst of it Caz gets a phone call from Mark. Caz laughs and smiles continuously as they talk (the first time I'd ever seen her smile so broadly) as they make plans for the weekend. She tells him, "Dr. Hollman is here, and I'm feeding Semantha." He apparently says, "I love you," and she says, "I love you, too." Caz continues to play with Semantha's feet following Semantha's lead and putting them to her mouth now and then to Semantha's absolute delight.

After the feeding of food, Caz changes Semantha on the changing table continuing to interact with her playfully. She says, "Semantha now recognizes specific people she sees every day. When I pick her up at day care, she definitely wants me specifically, like you said would happen. So, thanks. She doesn't yet recognize my mother who she doesn't see every day. She also sees Mark almost every day."

Then she lays Semantha on a new quilt with a mobile on it and goes to prepare her bottle of milk. Semantha plays by herself for quite a while still interested in catching her feet. She reaches for the mobile toys and randomly catches one as Caz is re-entering the bedroom with the bottle.

I comment, "Semantha is enjoying independent play. She reaches and holds on to a toy, and her interest in her feet makes her roll back and forth now almost as if she could turn over." Caz adds, "She plays for half an hour by herself in the crib in the morning." I respond, "Independent play is another accomplishment!"

Then Caz picks her up and holds her in her arms giving her a bottle of six ounces of milk. She says, "Sometimes she drinks only two ounces; sometimes the whole thing. She is sleeping through the night regularly."

"Wow, a change. Great job the two of you!" Caz grins broadly.

Now and then Semantha stops as if she doesn't want more but then complains and does want more after all. Caz follows her lead. "Okay. You want more. That's okay with me." With some of these bouts of complaints Caz says, "I know life is hard, eating, sleeping, and pooping."

What Does Caz Learn Playing with Semantha?

This is a fine example of how the love of another (Mark) serves such a supportive role to Caz that she can be more giving and responsive to her baby. Like Caz, you may also learn how you have become a responsive person your baby relates to, even after a separation for day care. You may also find your baby enjoys patient feeding and independent play as she reaches her fifth month.

∽

It's important to recognize your very particular importance to your baby's sense of security as well as her feeling your enjoyment in your interactions with her that are building her self-esteem. You may also find that as your baby enjoys your patient feeding, she is not only actually being well-nourished but well-loved. She is now more capable of independent play because *you* have given her the loving confidence she needs to feel secure on her own.

Being Social and Interactive with Your Baby

What Do Researchers Have to Say about Your Six-Month-Old?

At six months old, your baby's mouth is her focus for exploration and discovery, and she loves to hear the sounds she can make. She is very social and interactive and physically even more capable—so play is more important than ever.

Optimal Excitability

According to Stern (1985), each infant has her own level of pleasurable optimal excitability when playing. Below this level, an experience becomes uninteresting, and above this level, the excitation is too much. The optimal level of excitation and stimulation varies for each baby. Additionally, your infant will regulate her own level of excitation by looking away or other gazing and facial reactions. Your infant shuts out stimulation that feels above her optimal range, and she seeks out or invites new or higher levels of stimulation when the level of excitation is too low.

Thus, there is mutual regulation between you and the baby—just as there has been and will be in the future. As mentioned previously, this is an early coping function so that your baby can discover that her caregiver will be a regulator of her levels of excitation—further enabling her to self-regulate her emotions and stimulation (Stern 1985).

Why Do Mothers Play Empathically?

Functional magnetic resonance imaging techniques or fMRI is a brain scanning technique which measures blood flow to various parts of the brain as they are activated. These techniques have demonstrated why mothers play so empathically with their six-month-olds:

> fMRI techniques . . . investigate the neurobiological basis of empathy in mothers with children aged between six and twelve months. . . . During these experiments, mothers were instructed to actively imitate or to feel empathy for pictures of their own or of an unknown child. Pictures were divided in distinct groups according to infants' facial expressions (joy, distress, ambiguous, and neutral). The fMRI data showed that when mothers felt empathy with infants' emotional expressions, this significantly activated large clusters of the mirror neuron areas and of the limbic system. Furthermore, these areas were more active (particularly in

the right hemisphere) when the mothers felt empathy with their own child. This may be the result of the increased maternal effort to understand their own children's emotions in order to interact effectively with them (i.e., helping her in distressing situations). (Ammaniti and Trentini 2009, 550)

The study goes on to conclude that these mirror neurons could play a big part in maternal responsiveness during a baby's first year (550). When your baby still has not developed the ability to talk—yet has more social and physiological needs—*your* body and mind are also developing and changing to adapt to his needs.

Proprioceptive Feedback

Social play is made up of exaggerated, repeated actions with variations. These repeated actions are allowing your baby to learn about self-caused and other-caused events in play. Theorists call it *proprioceptive feedback* when these repeated actions are carried out over and over again.

It is important to understand that proprioception is an awareness of the position in space of the rest of the body relating to any other body part. "Proprioceptive information is essential to the normal functioning of the body's mechanical control system and is normally acquired unconsciously from sense receptors in the muscles, joints, tendons and the balance organ of the inner ear" (Medical Dictionary 2020).

So, when your baby brings his thumb up to his own mouth, both volition (the baby is doing this by his own will) and proprioception are involved. But if your baby doesn't yet know the game when you introduce patty-cake or clap your baby's hands for him—then proprioception but not volition will be experienced.

Thus, with volition and proprioception the infant can sense self-willed action as well as interactions initiated by others. These social developments are taking place inside of your six-month-old as he attempts to play with you, his toys, and others around him. In simpler words, the infant is learning about self-caused and other-caused events in play.

Interpersonal Growth

Another thing to keep in mind as your growing baby plays is that, according to Stern (1985), in the sixth month the baby is no longer mostly engaged with social behaviors that bear on her physical needs—sleep and hunger. She is now becoming a social creature, ready and hungering for communication and interaction. By six months, she is more interpersonally oriented, or social, than ever before. When you play with your baby, continue to mark your tones with a raised, exaggerated pitch, and simplified syntax to stimulate your infant. Also continue to exaggerate your gaze behaviors along with your baby's interest in doing so.

Emotional and Motor Memory

When you play with your six-month-old from one day to the next, you may wonder if your baby remembers the affective and motor play you have previously introduced.

To answer this question experimentally Nachman and Stern (1983) made six- to seven-month-old infants laugh with a hand puppet that moved, "spoke," and played peekaboo (disappeared and reappeared). When the infants were shown the puppet a week later, the sight of it made them smile. This response is considered "cued recall" because the sight alone of the unmoving, silent puppet made them smile; in other words, it activated an emotional experience. Further, they smiled at the puppet only *after* the game experience. Cued recall for an emotional experience seems not to have to await the development of language. This shouldn't be surprising to psychoanalytic theorists, who have always assumed that emotional memories are laid down from the first moments, or at least weeks, of life (McDevitt 1979; Stern 1985, 93–94).

Another study that shows how good your six-month-old's memory is was done using music. According to Brazelton (1969), a baby that liked music could indicate when the volume was too loud by fussing. She would also feel positive when her mother went to fix it. The baby seemed to associate the happiness in the volume change with her mother's going to a particular place to change it. "On one occasion, [a mother and baby listened as] a baby cried on the radio. To [the] mother's surprise, [the baby] . . . puckered and began to cry, too. . . . She was sensitive to the moods of other babies and imitated the other infant's laughter as well as his crying" (154). In other words, she remembered or recalled these differences! This baby also clearly remembered playing peekaboo. "When her father took his hands away abruptly, [the baby] jumped, as if she were caught up in the game completely. After several games, her excitement built up with squeals, laughing out loud, and bouncing her body" (154). The baby remembered what would happen as the game continued.

Brazelton (1969) describes another example of an active baby teaching himself how to crawl by remembering that when he integrated leg and arm movements on the same side over and over, he found he should bring the opposing leg and arm along. With repeated trials, he recognized right away how his limbs worked. He had the ability to store this recognition for repetition. Further, he fussed when his mother interrupted his play and protested until she replaced him on his belly on the floor so he could continue his activity. At the same age that he was teaching himself to creep, this baby liked the "come and get me game." If he saw a parent starting toward him, he reacted with a happy squeal—remembering this action—and would push himself forward to get away as fast as he could. He played the game repetitively.

The Core Self

In Stern's (1985) terms, by this age the infant recognizes what he refers to as a core self and a core other—the mother. It is no wonder why your relationship with your little one is growing and developing.

Stern similarly discusses that babies can integrate different attributes of their core self. The self who acts, the self who feels, and the self who perceives her own body all get assembled, which is a form of memory (98). With these integrated memories, the core self is organized by the seventh month (99). This integration and organization can occur because the infant is interacting with another person who helps her to regulate her experiences during games—such as "peekaboo," "I'm gonna getcha," and retrieval games—all of which involve the baby wanting to be the center of attention (105).

Infant Development

The Sensory World

As your baby examines new objects with all his senses—including taste—you can build on his sensory experiences. Babies transfer what they feel or touch to what they see, and vice versa, because they are cross-modal. This means they delight in what they learn in one sensory modality and transfer it to another sensory modality. This is why it's so important to stimulate all of their senses. When stimulating babies, they like constancy as well as variety (Gopnik, Meltzoff, and Kuhl 1999, 87).

Your Baby's Perception of Relationships

Babies now realize that one thing is related to another. They have discovered the physical distance between not only two objects, but two people. You may even notice your baby crying (communicating with you) if you increase this distance more than he wants. Remarkably, your baby can also now understand when something can be "inside, outside, on top, above, next to, underneath, or in between something else" (Van de Rijt, Plooij, and Plas-Plooij 2019, 217).

Movement in Relationships

How fascinating it is that your six-month-old baby now understands that there is a relationship between others' movements. If two people walk separately, your baby notices that there is a relationship. How does this capacity translate into play? Your baby has discovered that she, too, can create relationships. She understands she can coordinate the movements of her body, limbs, and hands so that they work together. With this understanding, she is able to do more things with her toys as she plays—with you or independently. As your baby sees and plays with relationships, she finds her own unique way to change her behaviors. Isn't it startling to realize your little baby can now perceive so many kinds of relationships? (Van de Rijt, Plooij, and Plas-Plooij 2019, 219).

Understanding the Relationship between Things

With all of these changes, by six months old, a baby's world of play has expanded exponentially. Understanding the relationships between things makes babies aware of the world in new ways. Your baby may now put their toys on, in, beside, or under things; throw them out or over things; pull toys through something; take things apart; or even grasp the relationship between sounds, words, and events. So, a fun and great way to play is to talk to your baby often, calling things by names.

However, it's not only with vocal sound making but with physical sound making that babies continue to understand relationships, whether it's due to your initiatives or the baby's. When your baby bangs something, it may fall to the floor—due to his own initiative. Remember that with all this playing activity, he continues to explore relationships (Van de Rijt, Plooij, and Plas-Plooij 2019, 221, 223, 224)!

Solidifying Object Permanence

As you can see, playtime slowly evolves as your child ages. For example, you can still play peekaboo, but in new ways. You should also remember that although peekaboo has been fun for a while, it's now very important. It stimulates your child's growing memory, teaching her that things aren't gone just because she can't see them.

Socially Designed Behavior

Just to keep some perspective, I will divert from six-month-olds momentarily to give you an advance notice of what happens next. According to Stern, your six-month-old is developmentally designed to be social at this stage of his development:

> After six months the infant changes again and becomes fascinated by, and proficient in, manipulating external objects; coordination of limbs and hand-to-eye have improved rapidly, and an interest in inanimate objects sweeps the field. When in physiological and affective equilibrium, the infant becomes relatively more engaged with things than with people. So, it is in between these two shifts at two and six months of age that the infant is relatively more socially oriented. This short period of intense and almost exclusive sociability results both from default and design. (Stern 1985, 72)

This is an important reminder to enjoy this time at six months when your baby craves interactive play with you. By next month your baby will also increase his ability for independent play.

Novelty

Returning to the sixth-month-old, this, then, is the time for repetitious facial displays and body-touching games. For example, the game "I'm going to get you" (with tickling, walking fingers up and down the infant's legs and torso, landing with a chin tickle) can be played over and over. Each finger march can be different from the previous one in speed, suspense, and vocalizations. "The longer the caregiver can introduce an optimal amount of novelty into the performance of each successive round, the longer the infant will stay entranced" (Stern 1985, 73, 74). Don't let this short time of increased sociability leave without taking full advantage!

Bonding with Mother

Infants as early as two months—and certainly by six months—understand temporal events during play. By this I mean that infants act as though two events sharing the same chronological structure belong together. They recognize voice, movements, and expressions that share common timing go together. This suggests strongly that when a mother plays with her infant, the baby recognizes that the patterns of sounds, sights, and touches coming from himself and from his mother are separate—each with their own single, temporal structure (Stern 1985, 85). Thus, babies are very sophisticated in their ability to differentiate their own actions from those of others when they play; they can identify the source of interpersonal interactions.

In fact, by two or three months of age the infant can experience changes in her mother's facial expressions as being from that specific mother—not several entities. So, by six months your baby is playing actively with her clearly distinct mother—you!

Interpersonal Actions:
Associating Acts with Results

Six-month-olds enjoy the standing position. But how do they get the feeling of its importance so early? Do they associate their desires to stand with the results they get when helped to get in the standing position? Does the baby want to imitate others or is there an inborn drive to be upright? Brazelton (1969) suggests that since the baby shows so much enthusiasm to be stood up in early months, there must be an inborn urge for satisfaction from this upright position.

At the same time, babies know how to play to get the attention of the parent they want. While "dada" is one of the first vocalizations an infant can make, it is quickly associated with play and pleasure in learning. On the other hand, if "mama" seems to come out first when a complaint is heard, according to Brazelton, the mother will relieve the reason for the complaint more often. Your six-month-old can now associate his playing with results in a clever way. He may call to his mother from another room, and she might hurry to see if he's in distress, but instead he might be lying on his back grinning—understanding that he regained her attention successfully. Associating this vocal action with a result is quite clever indeed!

Remembering Past Play

Evoked memories also occur when a baby is alone, remembering what went on with another person.

> For instance, if a six-month-old, when alone, encounters a rattle and manages to grasp it and shake it enough so that it makes a sound, the initial pleasure may quickly become extreme delight and exuberance, expressed in smiling, vocalizing, and general body wriggling. . . . [This is] not only the result of successful mastery . . . but also the historical result of similar past moments. (Stern 1985, 113, 114)

So, your little six-month old's memory is growing in many different ways. He remembers you as his distinctive mother, what to expect during and after play, and is organizing his core self. His growing social abilities need your regulation, as he may become tired or distressed, but are a fun and important way for you to continue learning what your baby's optimal levels of excitability and interaction are. Your play with your baby is only becoming more important as these developments all continue and deepen in coming months.

Playtime Suggestions

- Put your six-month-old in front of a mirror and play peekaboo with him, using his own hands and face. From six to eight months old, your baby still does not recognize himself! In addition, he might not recognize your reflection, thinking the mirror shows another woman with another baby. (However, studies show that a six-month-old baby will still react either positively or negatively to a mirror image of his mother based on his attachment to her. If his reaction is favorable, it indicates his attachment is positive. If the baby rejects the reflection of his mother, then something going on is negative.)

- Similarly, if the person is the baby herself, she reacts as she does to her mother, that is positively if there is a positive attachment. It's as if the baby sees the mother in the picture of herself (Kernberg 2006, 44).

- Take a favorite toy and cover it with a blanket. Ask your baby, "Where did it go?" and see if she tries to pull the blanket away. If she does, clap and praise her grandly. Then see if she'll put the blanket back on and make her own discovery.

- If your baby enjoys a well-supported baby swing then place him in it, saying "hello" as he swings toward you and "good-bye" as he moves away. You'll see how quickly he picks up on how different sounds have different meanings.

- When you pick up your baby's toys, call them by name. She will quickly learn to recognize the names of his favorites, such as ball, baby doll, book, and pacifier.

- Hold two objects in front of your baby and call out the name of only one of them. See if your baby tries to point to or grab at the toy you name. If correctly identified, clap and smile.

- Name body parts for your baby, pointing to each and saying its name. Repeat this with nose, mouth, eyes, ears, hands, and fingers.

- Enjoy hand play by showing your baby how to play patty-cake. Start by doing the hand motions yourself as he watches. Then, move his hands in the same motions. After he has some understanding of the game, hold him in your lap and move his hands in the clapping motions from behind.

- When your baby makes a sound or facial expression, follow her lead and parrot the sound or expression. Imitate her. Next, make your own sound and try to get her to imitate you. She might not catch on right away, but she'll eventually follow your lead. When this happens, give her positive feedback by smiling and clapping.

- Point out colorful objects on the page of a book. If a red ball is shown, point to the ball and repeat what it is. The next time you read the book, repeat this action. After you finish reading the words on the page, ask her where the red ball is. If she doesn't point it out, place her finger on the ball. Reinforce this word recognition by praising her if she touches the ball without your help. Even if she can't do that, tell her she's great.

- Playing on the floor is fun. Put various toys around your baby while he is doing tummy time so that he can practice reaching, grasping, and mouthing toys of different colors and textures.

- Offer baby-safe kitchen gadgets. Set out measuring spoons, whisks, small pots or pans, and wooden spoons for your baby to play with.

- Try giving your baby stacking cups, baby gyms, teethers, ball rattles, or rainbow stackers (plastic, circular doughnut shapes on a rod).

- Spoon play during meals is great at this age. Start with your baby's spoon below the table or highchair tray, as close to vertical as possible without spilling food everywhere. Quickly and carefully bring it up and gently place it in your baby's mouth as you say, "Rocket landing on the moon." You can also say, "Here comes the racing speedboat," or, "Whale swimming in the ocean," by using an up-and-down bobbing motion. Another fun idea is to make a "chug-a-chug whoo-whoo" sound as you bob the spoon along, transforming it into a fascinating choo-choo train.

- Sit cross-legged on the floor with your baby facing you. If he can't yet sit on his own, prop a pillow behind him. Then sing this song to any tune you like, acting out the commands as you come to them:

    - Clap, clap, clap your hands

    - Clap your tiny hands.

    - Clap, clap, clap your hands

    - Clap your tiny hands.

    - Stomp, stomp, stomp your feet.

    - Pat, pat, pat your head.

    - Rub, rub, rub your tummy.

To review, six-month-olds play with their empathic mothers in the delightful social interactions they co-create. The more varied stimulation they receive, the more mastery results. But remember, there is an optimal excitability before the infant gets tired or distressed. Monitor your baby's optimal midrange level of activity closely so that you can relate and engage well together. Being this socially interactive with your baby reaps great rewards in your relationship.

An Illustration of a Mother and Six-Month-Old Baby at Play

Mommy: "Let's give everything a name today. This is a truck. This is a ball. This is your giraffe." (Each time the mother holds up the toy.)

With each naming, the baby looks at the object and wiggles his hands and feet with excitement. Sometimes he grabs the object and the mother waits while he investigates it before suggesting another toy.

Mommy: "Let's name the parts of your body. Ooh, your little nose. (Mother taps the tip of baby's nose.) Oh my, this is your mouth that opens and closes. I'm going to look inside. Ooh, there's your tongue. See my tongue? We can imitate each other."

The baby is delighted with the mother's voice as well as each body part she names.

Mommy: "Here are my eyes. Here are yours. We have different color eyes. Watch me blink my eyes. Sometimes you do that, too. If you look close up with those beautiful eyes you have, you see the toys so clearly. If I point far away, things are a bit blurry."

Of course, the baby doesn't understand all the Mommy is saying, but her constant movement of arms and legs shows her excitement and increasing curiosity.

A PLAY SESSION

Seventeen-year-old Lee picks up Gabriella, hugs her, and lifts her a little bit in the air. Lee seems to be enjoying Gabriella very much and Gabriella is responsive to her, smiling happily. Then Lee goes to a pile of bibs and goes about choosing one. I say, "Gabriella seems bigger."

Lee says, "It's only been a few days."

I say, "No. It's been two weeks. Time passes quickly. How long her hair is getting, and it's your color."

Lee smiles appreciably.

Lee sits and puts Gabriella on her lap facing me. Gabriella has a ready smile as soon as I smile at her. She is a happy yet quiet baby. She makes no sounds.

Lee volunteers, "Gabriella is almost sitting up. If I put Gabriella on her back, she rolls over and starts to try to sit up."

I say, "Won't it be interesting when she can fully sit up—how the world will look so different to her."

As we're talking our attention is very much focused on the baby who is mouthing her fingers and moving her tongue in and out of her mouth a lot. She smiles readily but is still quiet. Lee and I are quietly watching Gabriella together.

Lee says, "She'll be president someday."

I say cheerfully, "Maybe! Next year you'll be able to vote."

Lee says, "No, because I don't have papers. My parents got the papers in 2004 and have to wait until 2009 to be citizens. When they are citizens, then I will be, too. Gabriella is already is a citizen because she was born in the U.S."

Lee says, "I fed her bananas and cereal before. She eats fruits and cereal now."

She offers her the pacifier. The baby takes it with first one hand, then the other as well. The pacifier is on a string around her neck.

I say, "Is she able to get it by herself?"

Lee says, "Yes," and offers it to Gabriella again who takes it and bites on it.

"She seems to bite and suck."

I say, "Oh, and how is her teething? You told me about it on the phone."

"The baby has a white line on her gum but no teeth coming through yet."

She notices Gabriella squirm a bit, and Lee says she thinks she's getting tired. She takes the cap off her bottle and cuddles her and puts her in a feeding position. The baby takes the bottle, and Lee helps her put her hands around it while also holding it. The baby is looking at me. Lee says to her, "Not so fast." The baby is sucking quickly. Lee says she gives her six ounces now. "She's getting chubby."

After the baby is finished Lee says, "She'll get mad now when I take the bottle away from her." But the baby doesn't make a sound. Lee holds her against her chest and pats her back. She gets one quiet burp and says to the baby, "How about another?" She continues to pat her. "Just one more. No? You don't want to? Okay."

The baby continues to be our focus. Lee says, "She's so friendly."

We continue to watch the baby. Again, I notice how well she holds on to the pacifier herself. Then I reach to the floor and pick up a very colorful rattle. The baby doesn't grab it. She stares at it solemnly. Lee says, "I think she's looking at the colors. They're so bright."

We watch to see what Gabriella will do. Eventually she reaches for it and puts both hands on it. It's kind of large for her, so Lee holds it steady from the bottom. Then Lee shakes it. Now for the first time, I hear the baby. She has a soft squeal of delight, and Lee and I laugh and repeat the sound.

Lee says, "She likes when I shake it and continue to do that." The baby squeals. The baby mouths the rattle and Lee says, "No, don't put it in your mouth."

The baby continues to do it and although Lee is saying don't do it, she's also putting it up to her mouth again and again, and the baby's tongue keeps coming in and out. Then she also spits up, and it goes down her bib and on to the floor. She tries to hold the baby and reach to clean it with some tissues but says it's hard. I say, "I'll do it" and wipe it up quickly.

Then Lee says how much she likes to hold Gabriella. I say, "I know. I see." She then starts to scratch her back softly and the baby arches her back and laughs. We laugh, too. Lee continues to do it, and the baby laughs. I say, "She's so ticklish."

Then Lee tickles her under her ear. Then she tries her feet, but the baby cries out and she stops. She does her back again and the baby laughs. Then the signal that it's time to go to class rings and Lee says, "I wish I could stay with her more. I don't want to go to math."

She lifts the baby and says, "Should I take you along? I wish I could but it's time for the nursery." She hugs her and gets up, saying to me, "Thanks!" and she's off.

What Does Lee Learn from Playing with Gabriella?

Lee is clearly becoming more confident and prouder of her baby's new movements and teething. She seems happy when she's with her, and the baby responds in kind. She's discovering how important she is to her baby and proud of their relationship. She doesn't want to leave her which is quite moving to hear. It's evident earlier that she really enjoys cuddling her baby, and the baby is so responsive. They have a lovely bond.

∽

How does this mother and baby compare to you and your baby at this stage? I suspect you, too, are feeling more confident as a mother and having the wonderful experience of seeing and feeling how important you are; in fact, you are central in your baby's life.

The Seventh Month

Observing More Independence *in* Your Baby

What Do Researchers Have to Say about Your Seven-Month-Old?

Your baby is now becoming more independent. You may even miss her earlier total dependence on you. But it's important to enjoy her growth and budding determination.

At seven months old, babies can look in a mirror and recognize that the reflection is *like* them; however, they don't know who it is. While they are not aware that other babies are or are not like them, it is clear that infants enjoy other infants. Babies often show a preference for other babies in a crowded room, watching and imitating them (Brazelton 1969). This is a great age to get your baby together with other children, as she can learn from them and enjoy seeing others her size.

When a mother manipulates toys so that they swoop in and out and speak and tickle, they take on her *vitality affect.* In other words, as the mother plays with a toy with actions, motions, and emotions, the infant's interest or vitality is heightened in the object. Once the mother does so and then withdraws herself from the play, the infant will continue to explore the toy alone as if the toy were almost animate. It's like the toy has become almost like it is a living being interacting with the baby in a social way (Stern 1985).

Interacting with babies in social ways now takes on increased importance. During the seventh to ninth months, intersubjective relatedness (relating with others mutually affecting each other) is added to a sense of oneself. This means that social relationships become even more significant as they add to your baby's sense of a core self that now interacts with others.

Additionally, empathy from you, the mother, is becoming a different experience for your baby. In the younger baby, empathic responses are felt as important, as a kind of bridging two minds, yours with your baby's. Now that your infant is grasping intersubjective relatedness, the emotional relationship with you, your "empathy, that process crucial to the infant's development" has a major impact on your baby's experiences (Stern 1985,125–126).

Empathy is of course the mother's ability to share and understand the feelings of her baby. If the baby laughs and the mother laughs in kind, the baby feels heard and understood. Similarly, mirroring facial expressions in a general way and repeating what your baby says, like "Da-Da," shows you are attentively understanding.

That is, your baby not only enjoys feeling understood by you, but experiences this as increasingly important to your relationship. This is an enlightening and warm experience for your baby. As we approach the eighth and ninth months, this will become more apparent. In the meantime, enjoy your baby's independent, as well as interpersonal, reactions.

Infant Development

Independent Actions

Your baby is now getting more independent as she creeps and crawls. According to Murkoff, Eisenberg, and Hathaway (2003), by seven months your baby may be able to:

- feed himself crackers

- initiate cooing and babbling on his own when he's happy

- initiate smiling when he's interacting with you

- sit without support on his own

- bear weight on his legs when he is held upright

- object when you take a toy away

- independently work to get an out-of-reach toy

- initiate looking for an object that dropped

- turn in the direction of a voice on his own

- babble combining vowels and a consonant

- initiate playing peekaboo by holding a towel in front of his face and then pulling it away

- creep or crawl on her own

- pass an object from one hand to another

- stand holding on to someone or something that she seeks out on her own

- pull up from sitting to a standing position with her own initiative

- get into a sitting position from her tummy

- initiate playing patty-cake, clap hands, and wave bye

- choose to pick up tiny objects

- walk on her own while holding on to furniture

- say "mama" or "dada" without distinguishing who they are

These new discoveries your baby is making are adding to her ability to explore the world around her with her own volition. For example, when she learns to sit up independently, she can also discover new uses for her hands. She can now wheel around in a moveable seat and lean over to pick up and retrieve dropped objects all by herself.

While some babies show a hand preference, most use both right and left indiscriminately. You may see even more development if your baby chooses to hold on to a *lovey* object as she moves around on her own. This is evidence of her attachment to a transitional object—her particular self-regulating or self-soothing object that reminds her of her mother.

Around this age you may also see your baby's independent determination to participate in her own feeding as she turns her head, shuts her mouth tightly, or grabs for a dish and spoon.

Playfully letting your baby direct feeding time makes it easier for the parent *and* is developmentally more effective.

In fact, seven-month-old babies are so independent that they can amuse themselves on their stomachs for thirty minutes at a time. They can handle a cluster of toy keys, rattling and mouthing each one, and they may love to finger strings of small beads of different shapes and textures. Babies learn to begin crawling through this independent determination! If your little one pushes a toy just out of reach, cries, and then realizes she has to solve the problem herself, she may scoot forward on her tummy to get it.

Motor Skills

As your baby's fine motor skills improve, he'll become more adept at grabbing, palming, and holding his toys. You will delight as your baby can reach for the toy he wants and have more careful control over it to shake, bring to his mouth, or even push it out his way.

Your baby may soon figure out how to clap hands of his own volition and will love playing games to refine this newfound skill— so now's the perfect time to reintroduce things like patty-cake.

Your baby is sitting up more securely and may be starting to creep or crawl, major milestones, so help your baby by giving him a safe practice space. This means it's babyproofing time if you haven't done so already. Make sure there are no little bits of things the baby might find on an unswept floor or wall plugs that need covering. It's of course important to watch your baby because it's so easy to see your baby close to bump into furniture if the space isn't large enough.

Don't forget that tummy time is still important at this age and that you can encourage even more movement with baby pushups.

You can also encourage baby pullups. Help him pull to stand up from sitting and let him bounce his legs a little before sitting back down. These exercises help train a baby's muscles and get him ready for future physical milestones.

Language

Your baby's vocabulary is also growing, and she may start to recognize familiar words. It's exciting to see which words your particular baby latches on to as she creates her language. Notice her interests and name those words in particular.

Cause and Effect

Your baby will also be really into cause and effect at this age. She'll love dropping, throwing, and banging just about anything—just to see what happens. If she's in her highchair and drops her spoon accidentally, she watches to see the effect on you. When you pick it up and clean it off so she can use it again, she notices. If, on the other hand, she's given a big spoon and pot and uses the spoon to hit the pot and enjoys the noisy effect, she's feeling a sense of agency.

Object Permanence

Your baby is still learning about object permanence, so she's realizing more and more that objects don't cease to exist when they are hidden. She'll enjoy covering her own face with a cloth and then removing it and reappearing with a big smile as well as watching you covering your face and then reappearing. She'll do this over and over with abundant giggles.

This concept of object permanence shows that your baby has reached a new milestone in her cognitive development with her new ability to think abstractly, a major milestone.

Language

Your baby's babbles and coos are his early attempts at communication. He not only responds to your voice tone, but he's also starting to piece together the way words form sentences. Many babies this age will respond to their names and start to associate words with familiar objects.

Playtime Suggestions

Give your baby plastic bowls or pots and pans, and she'll yelp with delight at the sounds she can make, again, demonstrating her interest in cause and effect (Halpern 2015, "How Should I Play with a 7-Month-Old?").

Now that your baby is sitting up and may be starting to creep or crawl, he'll often initiate play and enjoy having more control over his environment.

These days, your baby sees everything in the house as a potential toy and may actually have the skill to reach it! As mentioned above, this means it's the right time to keep up babyproofing. Be sure to get wires, pet food, breakables, and poisonous items out of your baby's reach.

While your seven-month-old is on her tummy, stand up and make noises or shake a favorite toy to get her to look up and lift her chest off the floor. You can also put a toy just out of her reach to stir her to move forward.

Help your baby to sit up supporting him with your hands or a pillow and giving him toys to explore while sitting.

Continue to play peekaboo; hide things behind a wall or blanket and then pop out and say "Boo!" holding the object in your hand. You can also hide a toy under a bucket or pillow and encourage her to find it.

Engage your baby in conversation by asking him a question and responding to his "answer." Narrate your day, read to him, and emphasize simple words for familiar objects. Ask, "Do you want a ball? There's your ball," as you give him a ball. Pause and wait for his response to see if he shows understanding at what is named.

As mentioned above, food itself is a game at this age. At seven months, babies will grab food with their fists and sometimes shove it toward their mouths. Parents.com suggests letting your baby practice—and make messes doing so. And Hello Motherhood shares that when "your baby can sit up unassisted, let her try to grab healthful bits of soft, cooked vegetables, always keeping a close eye to prevent choking" (Henry 2017).

As you play with your baby and watch him learn and develop, look for his budding sense of humor and emerging personality. Notice what your baby laughs at and what things he is drawn to (https://www.whattoexpect.com/first-year/month-by-month/month-7.aspx/).

Clap hands with your baby by having her clap her own hands and also clapping her hand against yours. Play patty-cake.

Create games geared around language. Keep it simple, to prevent your baby from getting frustrated. Lay out objects around your baby that you know he'll recognize. Then ask, "Where's the brush? the spoon? the doggy?" Praise him and cheer when he gets it right but smile and enjoy him even if he doesn't! Remember, there's no failure, ever, no matter what he does.

An Illustration of a Mother and Seven-Month-Old Baby at Play

Mommy: "Hi honey. Watch me hide."

Mommy hides behind a very large pillow.

While under the pillow, Mommy's face is hidden. Ask, "Where is Mommy? Can you find her?"

Give the baby a chance to react even if it's a few seconds before she does. If she finds you by moving the pillow, say, "You found me!"

If she doesn't find you, then Mommy says, "Look. Here I am!" as you come out from under the pillow.

Try it a few times smiling and laughing.

A PLAY SESSION

I surprise Caz at the door because she is barefoot wearing pajama bottoms and a sweatshirt. I come in to see Semantha is wide awake in her exerciser playing with the different toys on it and happily watching the cats.

Caz says, "Semantha is beginning to crawl, so I just had to vacuum."

I respond, "It's harder to have an almost crawling baby now. Good for you though for keeping track of anything on the floor that she might pick up. More work for you, but you're such a good mother to be careful for her."

I kneel down at Semantha's level, and she makes various sounds as if talking to me and reaching for the cats. Caz says just when Mark is around, she says "Da-Da." I wonder if she realizes the Da-Da is him. Caz doubts it, but says Mark thinks so, and she laughs.

Caz lets me know her mother's bipolar disorder is no longer in remission and she is hospitalized to readjust her medication. I empathize with her worry about her mother and appreciate her finding time to visit with her.

Caz does not have this disorder but has had periods of depression for which she is being treated as an outpatient. She says that her own medicine seems to have started to work because she's begun to read again, she's less anxious, and found pleasure in going out yesterday. She and Mark took Semantha to walk in the village. They saw a lot of people with babies who had the same idea. They also took Semantha to a barbecue. She says to Semantha, "And you were very good there, weren't you?"

Then Caz takes Semantha out of the exerciser and puts her on the floor in a sitting position. She puts a toy that has blinking color a little out of reach, and Semantha reaches for it but can't touch it. She reaches and reaches and then manages to put out her two arms and one leg in a crawl position, but the other leg stays tucked under her. She can't quite make it into a crawl, but she does retrieve the toy. We encourage Semantha. I say something like, "Go for it, you can do it." She enjoys the attention and playful encouragement.

We continue this kind of play for a while until Caz decides she's had pleasurable exercise and needs to be changed.

On the changing table, Semantha is reaching for anything in sight. Caz shifts gears and decides, instead of a new diaper, it's time for a bath and more play. She sets up the plastic tub in the large bathtub and places Semantha in it comfortably because she likes the water. Caz and Semantha play with bath toys together, smiling at each other as they give and take different plastic objects moving them in and out of the water.

After the bath she enjoys dressing her in a pretty outfit and sits with her on the floor to play. She takes out a rainbow stacker to play with. Semantha knocks it down and reaches for the different circles. Like earlier, Caz puts one out of reach and Semantha works so hard to get into the crawling position but just can't get one leg out from under her and ends up frustrated on her belly. Caz puts her in the crawling position again, but she can't hold it. Then play turns to some complaining without tears and Caz sees Semantha is tired out from her crawling attempts and is hungry, so Caz goes to get a bottle.

As she waits for her bottle, Semantha is easily distracted by a toy with plastic circles that I give her. She bangs two circles together and makes a noise. But intermittently cries out looking for her mother and the bottle. Then Caz sits on the floor with Semantha in her arms and gives her the bottle. Caz looks soberly at Semantha the whole time and Semantha looks at her and now and then and also at me and around her. I can see that it's hard for Caz to stay focused only on her baby because she is also worried about her mother's mental illness and hospital stay.

Semantha's main focus is her mother. She reaches with one hand for her hair and with the other hand holds on to Caz's pant leg. As she finishes drinking, she makes a little sound like she's had enough. Caz encourages her to finish it, so she takes a little more and then is done. It is time for me to go. Caz wishes me a good day. I reiterate I appreciate her working so hard to be a kind daughter and mother all at once.

What Does Caz Learn from Playing with Semantha?

Although Caz is clearly worried about her own mother's mental health it does not distract her too much from focusing on Semantha. I notice her distraction mostly when she's feeding Semantha and does not keep her eyes on her even as Semantha gazes at Caz, yet she also continues to watch Semantha's attempts at crawling patiently and is attentive when her focus shifts to hunger. Caz is becoming an attentive mother even when her family situation is challenging due to her mother's illness. Being an attentive mother and daughter is stressful, but Caz seems to be able to manage both without letting her own mother's struggle interfere with mothering Semantha, a tribute to her growing experience and resilience.

$\sim$

You may also find at times that you carry several roles such as mother and daughter and adult partner. It's hard to balance out being available for everyone and also finding time for yourself and your own needs. Mothers can get easily fatigued not only by their baby's constant needs even as they become more independent, but also by the stressors of everyday life. It's important to know when you need support from an adult partner or friend, so mothering doesn't become an overwhelming role but one that remains enjoyable and appreciated by those around you. Mothers need not only physical support with playing and caring for their baby but emotional support as well. This is crucial and should never be underestimated.

Strengthening Object Permanence *with* Your Baby

What Do Researchers Have to Say about Your Eight-Month-Old?

Your eight-month-old is probably sitting securely now and starting to creep or crawl, initiating play and gaining more control over what she does in her environment. With her fine motor skills increasing, she is better learning to grab, palm, and hold on to various toys. As you continue playing peekaboo, hide-and-seek, here and gone, and hello and bye-bye—you're strengthening your baby's sense of object permanence (the idea that things exist even when you can't see them). As mentioned in previous chapters, such fun games also help with brain development. In fact, you have seen versions of many of the ideas you will see in this chapter in previous chapters. However, notice that the games and forms of play are never *exactly* the same—they are changing and growing with your child. Keep this in mind as you watch your child explore new aspects of play, and you can discover even more ways to spark your child's imagination and curiosity.

Interesting research has been done about eight-month-old babies and grammar. They learn grammar at the same time as they are learning words—even before they start speaking. Researchers in France have found that babies this age can distinguish between parts of speech that serve functions like articles, pronouns, and prepositions and words of content such as nouns, verbs, and adjectives. French researchers took a sample of 175 eight-month-olds and who listened to four minutes of made-up language. By observing how long the babies looked at displays of made-up words, they were able to evaluate word preferences. So, grammar is now understood to be part of the eight-month-old's world sooner than was thought (McNamara 2020).

The researchers discovered that the babies were more interested in new content words, the nouns, verbs, and adjectives like ball, run, or pretty than newly shown function words, articles (a, an, the), pronouns (he, she, it, etc.), and prepositions (on, over, around, etc.). Babies use these words to form rudimentary understandings of grammar (McNamara 2020).

What does this research mean to you and your baby? Keep talking and sharing with your baby using varied language. What you say matters to your baby as they learn to speak, but remember that, whatever you say, say it with pleasure as you are talking smiling and playing with your baby.

Infant Development

Language

As your eight-month-old's vocabulary continues to grow, she will recognize more and more words, so encourage games around language. Name things in the world around you, in picture books, and in photos. Keep in mind that language is verbal as well as nonverbal. Your baby may be able to wave bye-bye, nod her head yes and no, and communicate in other nonverbal ways.

Does your baby understand the sounds that make words have meanings? Sometimes yes and sometimes no. See if you can figure it out! When your baby babbles, she may just be practicing a new or old sound, but she may be imitating your words with comprehension. "No" is a word that she may understand for example, but also remember she comprehends much more of what she hears than she can say.

Remember that when you point to something and give its name, she may point as well without knowing that the name goes with the object. Some babies' first full words don't come until they're ten to fourteen months old, and some babies' come much earlier. Often at this age, however, your baby will be using syllables—alone and in combination—to represent objects, such as "ba" for bottle, "ba-ba" for bye-bye, or "daw" for dog. Pay keen attention to understanding that may be going on before your eyes without you realizing it, because, as noted above, your baby can understand what is said before she can say it. She'll probably follow simple commands, such as "Wave bye-bye," "Give me a bite," or "Kiss Mommy."

Here are a few tips from Murkoff, Eisenberg, and Hathaway (2003) to encourage language development:

- Talk slowly, giving your baby a chance to pick out words separately.

- Emphasize individual words and simple phrases by narrating what you are doing.

- Pronouns are probably still confusing, so say proper names like "*Mommy* is feeding you bananas." (386)

Talk to your baby about everything you do—from diapering to bathing to strolling in the park. Build a repertoire of simple rhymes and songs that you repeat over and over. Remember to wait for a response when you are talking to your baby; he has a lot to say. Introduce new concepts and see how they go over with your baby, such as the pillow is soft, the block is hard, and soap is for washing.

Encourage discovery if your baby uses a toy in an unconventional way, and don't hesitate to go along with the new game with words.

Language is interactive, so remember to listen before you speak in order to hear what your baby is trying to communicate. Let your baby interrupt adult conversation; she doesn't know that it isn't polite, and you don't want to reject or shut down her lively communications.

Notice that your baby may use syllables based on the sound something makes to name it—like "wa-wa" for a whirring truck, which could easily escape your notice.

Movement

Your baby is now more capable of not only picking up an object but also transferring objects from one hand to another.

The pincer grasp, using an index finger and thumb to hold something, is also more developed. This allows new kinds of play as well as picking up small bits of food on the highchair table.

Object Permanence

Recognizing that what isn't seen is still there is getting very well-established which increases your baby's ability to take his own initiative in play and also feel a sense of security knowing that when you walk around the corner, you will come back.

Social Interaction

It's exciting to see triadic interactions. Babies are now interested in watching several people interact and she happily joins in. She can play chase with Mommy and Daddy or give and take objects with two different people. She can also pass objects from hand to hand. Her social world is expanding exponentially at the same time as her capacity to hold attention is longer, and thus it's easier to stay social for increasing amounts of time.

Movement

Your baby gets around much more easily now which also means he can explore and make new discoveries on his own. With this facility for movement such as crawling, scooting, and maybe holding on and cruising, his world has expanded tremendously. He is able to follow directions as he moves to different rooms and places even outside. Mobility is his new adventure including chasing and being chased.

Relationship with Mother

Just as you've done in previous months, show your baby herself in the mirror and then her mother in the mirror. Remember the baby won't recognize herself, but she will react to the baby and the reflection of her mother based on her attachment experience with her mother. If the baby reacts to the mirror images with excitement and pleasure, it is an indication that this is how she feels toward her mother. This is even true if the baby does not yet recognize herself; infants will respond positively to their own reflections when their relationship with their mother is secure.

While young infants literally take the image to be another child [when they see themselves in the mirror] and display a positive emotional response, it is again a similar affirming type of interaction described in positive experiences with the mother (Kernberg 2006).

Observe how your baby's reactions do or do not change as your relationship grows and as the months go by.

Playtime Suggestions

- Put a bunch of objects around her and ask, "Where's the ball? the spoon? the bunny?" You may see her pointing, which is another game, showing that she understands direction. Don't forget to point to things yourself, naming objects as she follows your direction.

- Cause and effect is delightful to your baby now. Find things for him to see, like the flicking of a switch to turn the light on, and then have him try it. Then, turn the switch again and let him see the light go off. Watch his expression as he tries faucets and doorbells, too.

- Your baby's interest in dropping things (that you retrieve to reinforce object permanence), throwing things, and banging pots and pans is continuing to grow. An eight-month-old does this repeatedly as she explores her sense of object permanence.

- Mirrors are great for playtime, as your baby is slowly discovering that his reflection is his own. Name and point at him in person and then in the mirror and see if he gets it.

- Repetition is important, as is novelty. Many games won't work the first time you play them, because your baby's attention span will vary a lot depending on his mood and temperament. Sometimes he'll enjoy a game for as long as twenty minutes, but often you'll need to change the game every five minutes or so. Overall, his attention span is growing though, so don't give up too soon. You'll know your baby is having fun when he turns toward you, smiles, giggles, and laughs. When he squirms away, arches his back, looks away, or cries, pay attention and stay attune to him; he's had enough and wants to change what you are doing.

- Because your baby's capacity to transfer objects back and forth from hand to hand is increasing, make this movement into a game. Cheer when he succeeds. Also promote his newfound pincer grasp skill by encouraging him to pick up small, safe objects like O-shaped cereal, cooled boiled rice, pieces of banana, peas, and corn to enhance hand control.

- Continue letting your baby investigate his environment by giving him a lot of new things to examine, like pots and pans and kitchen utensils. Then watch him bang them, bite them, throw them away, and retrieve them.

- At this age, babies are good at interacting with more than one person at the same time. You can play peekaboo or throw a ball with several others and then watch your baby try to get herself back into the center of attention.

- Your eight-month-old enjoys imitating you. Make funny faces, put your hands in the air, or shake your head, and then watch your baby attempt to do the same. This is also a great way of interacting with your baby!

- Your baby will love to take two objects and bang them together, hold them up to the light, squint at them, bang them separately on the table, and bang them together on the table. He may even explore hitting the objects with different hands and observing whether they make the same sound. Help him out by passing him objects that make interesting sounds—such as hollow containers, metal spoons, and rolls of paper towels.

- Pay attention to tactile sensations. Your baby may love to play with cooked linguini, plastic keys, cloth with different textures, and cardboard boxes that open and close. Let her open and close drawers (being careful they don't fall

out on her or pinch fingers), as this can also be a fun
sensation around eight months of age.

- Create obstacle courses for your baby if he is crawling,
  scooting, or even walking. He may enjoy the challenge of
  moving things on his own after you demonstrate the course.
  Then, put things in his way and watch him navigate around
  them, increasing his motor strength and control.

- There are multiple variations of peekaboo that will help
  increase your baby's sense of object permanence. Hold up
  a cloth between your face and your baby and ask, "Where
  is Mommy?" repeatedly. You can also hide behind a door
  and make your baby push it open to find and see you. Or,
  gather a selection of hats behind the sofa and pop up and
  down—wearing a different hat each time. You can then
  put the hats on her and have her take them off and on.

- Babies are intrigued by balls and how they move. You'll
  get a big giggle when you toss a ball up in the air and
  let it hit the floor while you make a silly sound, like
  "Whoops!" You can also roll a soft ball toward your baby
  and watch him grab and squeeze it. In time and with
  encouragement, he'll roll the ball back toward you.

- Once your baby is crawling, play chasing games. You can
  crawl behind her and then in front of her, letting her be
  both the pursued and the pursuer.

- Blocks can be some of the best toys for a child. At this
  young age, stack up blocks yourself and then show your
  baby how to knock them down. Build another tower and

see if he's caught on! You can also use small blocks to make fun objects that will entice your baby. Or, practice putting the blocks in a pot together—one at a time.

- If you have toys that can be taken apart and put back together again, this is the time to present them. Puzzles and interlocking toys are fun for an eight-month-old. Your baby will want to see how to take them apart and watch as you show how to put them back together again. She will soon learn how to put back them together again all by herself.

- Reading to your child is one of the best things you can do for him. It will help him with language development as he hears brand-new words with interesting sounds. And, of course, your baby will enjoy simply hearing your voice. Make it fun by giving the characters in the story different voices or sounds and then watch your baby's face. Eight-month-old babies love black-and-white books as well as colorfully vivid picture books. They also enjoy books that have textures on them as well as books with sounds. However you decide to do it, and whatever book you choose, you can't go wrong. So just grab a book, sit back, enjoy your tot, and watch him learn (Clayton 2011).

Enjoy this month before it escapes you. Your baby will undoubtedly reach new milestones, some more noticeable than others. Maybe he'll even master object permanence!

An Illustration of Parents and Eight-Month-Old Baby at Play

Mommy and Daddy are very intrigued now with their baby's remarkable ability to get around. She may be more or less adventurous with one parent more than another. She will look to one parent or the other if she is unsure of trying a new location. If she sees a grin, she'll venture forth more readily.

Daddy sets up an obstacle course with pillows, chairs, and little baby size tables for the baby to crawl around and under. He follows the best he can, sometimes changing direction to see if the baby follows him or continues on her own course.

Daddy: "Hi honey. I'm over here. Oops, now I'm over here. Can you find me? I see you. Do you see me?"

Mommy: "You're following Daddy, but what about me? I'm going to chase you, so you move even faster around everything in your path. Oh, it's so much fun seeing you laugh out loud."

These parents are aware their baby can interact with both of them at once and are enjoying family play.

A PLAY SESSION

Sixteen-year-old Viola arrives for the session and talks nonstop the whole time. Baby Joel is not in school today. I say that's fine. "It gives us an opportunity to talk about how you and he are doing."

She tells me. "This morning my mother asked to have Joel for the day, and she never ever asks, so I said yes."

I said, "How did it feel?"

"Well I don't like seeing all the other babies in the nursery and Joel isn't here."

"You miss him."

She tells me she does and to help out with those feelings she wants to show me pictures. She takes out her camera and I see him and say how cute he looks.

She says, "Yeah. He's doing so many things now. He holds on to the desk and stands for a little and he eats everything! He loves pasta. He isn't so interested in baby food any more like he knows there's a world out there. I tried him on the Enfamil again, but his poop was loose, so I can't do that anymore. He likes the soy milk better. He eats so much now. In the nursery, if I'm eating pasta, he sits in the chair and yells at me. Others ask what's wrong with him, and I say nothing. He just wants pasta. So, I give him two jars of food and then the pasta."

She tells me, "He's still not crawling, but he is slugging forward on his stomach and even on his back. He just reaches for things but doesn't like to move a lot. Also, he is sleeping through the night."

"You were so worried about that. Tell me how it's going."

"Well you have to listen to this whole schedule. I feed him then I put Vicks on his chest and back evenly. I hold him against my chest, so he feels really good. Then I read him a book. The same book every night. Then I put him in the chair and rock it with my foot. It's still for infants, but I do it. Then I put him in the crib with a blanket, so he has something to hug in the corner. And he sleeps the whole night. He goes to bed about 9 o'clock and wakes up about 8 o'clock if I don't go to school. My boyfriend, Caesar, loves Joel so much. They play together so well."

I say, "He's a really good dad."

"He is," she says. "He loves Joel more than anyone, more than he could love a girl. They like to wrestle with their feet. They are really good together. When Caesar is in a bad mood when he comes, he sees Joel's smile and he feels better."

"You've really created a great plan for Joel's sleeping. Great job for both of you!"

She goes on to say that Joel is shy. "He sees other people and smiles and then puts his head in my chest. My grandmother loves him. You should see the kisses she puts all over him. But Joel hugs me. He's my best friend. I remember in March I came to this school, and I didn't know anyone. Then it was summer, and I had no one except Joel."

I say, "You have become so attached to him."

"I have. I am so attached to him. When he gets older, I'll feel sad. I love him this age. He's so much fun to play with. I want him as a baby. He'll be one year in four months. Then he'll go to kindergarten and then he'll be older and won't want me to hug him. I wanted a momma's boy, and I got one. I know now what his cries mean, when he's hungry or needs to be changed. I like this age so much. Oh, one morning he woke up and said, 'mama.' He said it just like that."

I said, "And that felt so good."

"It did," she says. "He hasn't said it much again. It was just that day."

"I went back to my old school with Joel. Everyone came out to see him. They said he's so cute and they noticed his sneakers and hair and they said he's so adorable. I remember being pregnant in the school and no one knowing. One teacher said she knew because one day my stomach moved and I put my hand on it and she thought, 'Oh, she's pregnant.' So, she knew.'"

I ask her more about how it was this morning when her mother asked to take Joel. She said, "I told her, 'Oh and I have therapy and want Dr. Hollman to see Joel.'"

My mother said, "Do you want to take him then?"

I said she could have him because she never, never asks. She's working all the time. She plays with him sometimes and just makes these faces at him. But I just thought she should be with him. But it was really lonely on the bus and seeing all the babies in the nursery."

I say, "Next week you will be on vacation, so we won't see each other."

She says. "I know." She looks sad, but then shows me another picture of Joel as if that helps her know

I'll remember her and him even in our week's absence. This is a creative way to cope with her feelings. Then she adds, "He's nineteen pounds."

I say, "He has grown a lot. Next time we meet we'll see if he's grown even more. It will be great to see you again soon."

It's hard for her to say good-bye to me. We've formed a good connection that strengthens her self-worth as a mother and young girl. She feels close to me because she feels understood. So, I reinforce that our absence from each other will be brief, and I will surely be here again when she returns.

What Does Viola Learn from Talking with Me without Joel?

This was a unique opportunity to give Viola the attention she needs without sharing me with her baby. She clearly missed her baby but felt it was important for her mother to have some time with him because she doesn't often due to her hard work schedule. Viola liked my attention and interest in all her details about Joel. She doesn't get that often from her mother and seemed to relish it with me. I was glad to be there for her because she doesn't seem to be getting the mothering she needs, yet it doesn't prevent her from being a very attentive mother to her baby. Her feelings about not wanting her baby to get older made me consider that their mother-baby bond fulfills a need for closeness that the baby gives her when her own mother cannot.

Many mothers adore the baby stage because they enjoy the physical and emotional closeness. It's hard to feel you may have to give that up when actually, you don't. Instead the bond grows in new and important ways, and you will still feel close to your growing baby.

The Mutual Sharing of Mental and Emotional Interactions with Your Baby

What Do Researchers Have to Say about Your Nine-Month-Old?

Nine months is a fascinating time. There are many new milestone developments that can be easily missed as you are busy feeding, dressing, and playing with your baby. I will explain what researchers tell us about many new topics: joint attention; social referencing; sharing attention and intentions; sharing affective states; imitation; triadic interactions with the self, other, and an object; and the baby's growing cognition and affective awareness. Even discovering categories are coming to the fore influencing playtime. Let's look at each separately in order to grasp the full significance.

Joint Attention

By nine months your baby is sharing her attention with others frequently. The gesture of pointing is making an even bigger impact now as she follows *your* line of vision when you look or point at something. This ability to focus her attention on what you'd like is called *joint attention*, and it is a big milestone! Think first of the mother pointing. The infant must know to stop looking at the pointing hand and look toward the direction the pointing indicates. There is a target. What a discovery! Your baby is going beyond her egocentrism, appreciating another's line of regard, and detecting others' intentions.

These extraordinary feats mean *your baby knows another person has a mind*—which makes play even more complex. It is significant to note, however, that pointing gestures may not all be followed by the baby until she is fifteen months old, depending on how close the object is that is pointed to (Carpendale and Lewis 2008, 97).

Infants at nine months old can do even more than follow your line of vision when you point. After your baby's eyes reach the target, he will look back at you. He is using your feedback from the expression on your face to determine if he has isolated the correct target.

Although your infant isn't aware of his accomplishments, these are deliberate moves that will validate whether joint attention has been achieved and now is shared. It might also be helpful to point out that joint attention is part of intersubjective relatedness, which we discussed in the chapter on the seventh month (Stern 1985, 135). Intersubjective relatedness refers to your baby's ability to recognize others as separate and interact with them in a mutual way as mother and baby affect each other. It is the psychological relation between the mother and baby.

When your infant points by himself, his gaze will alternate between his target, like a toy, and your face until he sees that you have joined him with avid attention toward that particular focus, his favorite toy. How remarkable is that!

In the last month, you may also have noticed your baby reaching to his favorite object but checking back to your face to see if your reaction is new. This is a new form of communication between you and your baby. He is looking for feedback and shouldn't be ignored. Smile and join in the play.

Social Referencing

Another form of joint attention and social interaction that develops at about nine months is called *social referencing*. This happens when the infant looks toward a parent or caregiver for what to do when faced with an ambiguous event. Consider the results of the famous visual cliff experiment where the baby sees a transparent surface they must crawl on to reach their mother which looks like a vertical drop off, or the experiment with a baby eyeing a toy spider they might be afraid of also across a short distance from their mother. Both reveal how the baby is seeking the mother's facial reaction to guide the baby to decide whether to approach or avoid the situation. This behavior is attributed to nine months and beyond. Thus, in new situations, infants will look at their parents' faces in order to gauge an emotional reaction before they proceed. If the mother smiles, the infant is most likely to cross the visual cliff or play with an ambiguous toy while he is less likely if his mother frowns or appears uninterested (Carpendale and Lewis 2008, 85).

This requires that the infant and mother know they are attending to the same thing, something they both see in common. What a milestone that is! Both must be aware that they are attending to the same place or object. We have yet to clearly understand what precise social understanding is going on with joint attention, but these abilities will certainly enhance your baby's play.

Sharing Attention

We've talked about functions of pointing. Infants use pointing to initiate or make requests or to get someone to do something (e.g., "get that for me"). Pointing is thus used to get the adult's attention. That is, to *share* attention. This pointing might begin at nine months but will be further clarified by the baby's first birthday. Joint attention is a kind of sharing attention meaning the baby and mother are using their minds together to understand each other's intentions. Whether it's the mother or the baby leading the interaction to get the specific attention of the other, the important key here is that they are sharing minds (or sharing attention) and communicating to each other in a way the baby or mother understands the intention of the other vis-à-vis the pointing. This interrelationship is quite astounding when you realize the baby is only nine months old and cannot even use language yet.

Sharing Intentions

Researchers have determined that at nine months old your baby *intends* to communicate. Gestures, postures, actions, and other non-verbal vocalizations have already been displayed for months. The intention to communicate actively is an attempt to *influence* another person and *relate* to them.

Intentional communication occurs when a baby persistently attempts to communicate something until he is either successful or failure is clear. Because your nine-month-old is not yet talking, he may try to do this through alternating his eye contact between you and the goal. If he's not sure he's getting his communication across, he will begin exaggerating or changing his signals until his goal is achieved which is for you to understand what he's after.

Here is a great working definition of intentional communication:

Intentional communication is signaling behavior in which the sender [the baby] is aware . . . of the effect that the signal will have on his listener [the mother], and he persists in that behavior until the effect is obtained or failure is clearly indicated. (Stern 1985, 130–131)

In other words, your baby who can't yet speak is now capable of intending by using pre-verbal requesting. Hold out a cookie that your infant wants. Your infant will most likely reach out her hand with her palm facing upward, making grasping movements and looking back and forth to the targeted cookie and your face. She may even add a sound, like "Eh, eh," to indicate what she wants. This act infers that your baby attributes an *inner* mental state to you; then you know you have something, the cookie, your baby is interested in having. And it is an excellent example of intentional communication! As you comprehend your baby's intention through her gestures and sounds, she also understands your intention. "Intentions have become shareable experiences" that the baby may not actually be aware of (Stern 1985,131).

This *shared* moment of the relation between mother and baby can be extended to all kinds of play. Now peekaboo is understood as a shareable intention along with patty-cake, hand clapping, mirror looking, block building, and reading together.

It cannot be overemphasized how remarkable it is now that your baby is comprehending (in some way) *your mental state* (your mind and attitude) that involves "intentions and expectations" (131).

Sharing Affective States

Now we can focus on how mothers and babies share *emotional states*. When your baby is nine months old, notice the correspondence or similarity between his own affective (emotional) state of mind and the affective expression seen on another's face such as yours!

For example, if a baby is sad and upset because of several minutes of separation from his mother, a happy face may eventually appear when they are reunited. We can now conclude that this infant somehow makes a match between his feeling *within* him and the feeling seen "on" or "in" his mother, another person.

This is a match that researchers call *interaffectivity* (Stern 1985, 132). "Inter" refers to how these feelings exist *between mother and baby*. Isn't this an astounding sharing of emotions exchanged between you and your baby? How wonderful it is that you and your baby share feelings and emotions. This is the baby's most important or primary communication with you, a communication of emotions (133).

In fact, most play is a form of sharing emotions, such as ball playing, turning on switches, peekaboo, clapping, reading, hiding, and finding objects and people. There are emotions that are exchanged with each moment of play; it's not the ball rolling that's so significant, but that the baby reacts with such delight.

The thing that makes intersubjective exchange so impressive is that the mother and baby share emotions! When the baby says "ba-ba" for ball, the mother reacts with delighted pride at her baby's language development. They *share* excitement. Oh my! The mother and baby are sharing a momentous event with great feeling attached to it and each other.

In order to further envision this *mood sharing* event, think of a baby and mother's moods as they clap hands at the same time. You are witnessing not only new social skills but meaningful emotional exchanges—all with a new kind of awareness that enhances an understanding of the importance of play far beyond the aspects of language and motor development.

These moments of mood sharing are mutually created. Does this mean that mother and baby *need* "to share subjective experiences"? (135). That is, do mother and baby need to share emotions? Play takes on an astounding importance at this time, as curiosity and seeking to be stimulated to learn take on new dimensions. Such emotional sharing seems contagious for both mother and baby. It not only reinforces the baby's need for security but also for the goal of feeling attachment to the parent that involves the mother or father's fondness, sympathy, and affection for their baby.

For those readers who like being philosophical, we could even say your infant is now immersed in *existential* questions concerning the need to not be isolated but to be part of a group. This not only enhances pleasure but is important for survival.

Imitation

We have discussed in prior months how imitation is a primary focus of playing. But we do not know what the infant *feels* when he imitates his mother—or even what he feels when he sees himself in the mirror. When a baby imitates his mother pointing, as noted to occur in earlier months, he is beginning to follow his mother's gaze with emotion as he is actively engaging in social interaction.

Both following her gaze and turning into the direction of the gaze suggest that the infant knows there is something worth following. Your baby is attributing some level of meaning to his imitation of you (Carpendale and Lewis 2008). Your baby is beginning to appreciate what he does has meaning or is meaningful!

This suggests that imitation provides the basis for the infant to see other people as "just like me." This leads to some level of understanding of the functioning of others. That is, at this milestone infants may be somehow understanding that others have intentions just like they do (87).

Triadic Interaction

We have been talking about interactions between mother and baby, as well as between objects and baby. Now see how three—two people and one thing—can come together at the same time for interaction. Attention in triadic interactions (involving the self, other, and objects) develops from early dyadic interactions (involving parents and objects). This is hardly ever noted as impressive by parents when they are playing with their babies. However, it points to the emergence of language and new forms of interaction. We may notice when such interactions are missing rather than when they are present, as adults are used to triadic interactions.

Once again, this all suggests that infants have some "implicit" understanding of a "theory of mind—an understanding of the person with whom they interact" (Carpendale and Lewis 2008, 81). It is astonishing to realize infants are that capable of understanding others.

We are faced with wondering about the problem of knowing what infants understand about other people's intentions during joint attention such as pointing, gestures, gaze following and later, social referencing. There is mutual awareness in this play, but what infants exactly understand isn't clear. What do you imagine your baby understands when you observe him during his play? Is he interested in what's on your mind? Most likely! You, too, can be the researcher observing your particular baby! You, too, need to be interested in how your baby's mind is evolving by leaps and bounds.

Infant Development

Cognitive and Affective Awareness

Psychologists suggest that cognitive thought and affect (feelings, emotions, and moods) are linked. For example, what brings about the initial smile and then laughter when infants play? We know that from her earliest weeks—and certainly by nine months—a baby has a powerful regulating effect on the cognitive and emotional behavior of her mother, just as the mother has a significant regulating effect on the feeling, emotion, or mood and cognition of her baby. This cognition involves the baby's ability to think, experience, and use her senses as she interacts with you and the world.

But at what point do we attribute intentionality? When does a baby purposefully do something with the goal to get a reaction from an object or person? First, we need to distinguish between the effects of an infant's behavior and the *intended* effects of the infant's behavior (Carpendale and Lewis 2008, 200). It is believed that a baby must first learn how to intend with thought and emotion; only then can she begin to realize intentions. But what brings about this transition and when?

One possible answer is that when mothers assign meaning to their babies' expressions—such as a grimace or gesture—it influences the timing and manner of the baby's response by the way the mother reacts in turn. From here, the foundation of communicating through shared meanings between mother and baby begin to grow.

Surely, then, responses of thought and emotion are linked. A baby begins to understand the significance of his own actions and expressions only after his mother gives them meaning—in social situations (Carpendale and Lewis 2008, 201). In other words, it is the parent's actual treatment of the baby as a human person that is crucial to the baby's development as a human being. Your own interpretations or understandings of events become remarkably and significantly important in teaching your baby how to interpret or understand the intentions of those in the world around him.

Exploring Categories

Babies can now become aware of their ability to group things. What a revelation! A nine-month-old can discover that things look similar and make similar sounds, and that things might taste, smell, and feel the same. How does this affect play? You can help your baby *experiment* with categories during play; help him to observe and then compare the similarities between the things you put before him.

You may even notice his changing perception in the way he interacts with things that feel the same when touched. Infants recognize "*firmness, stickiness, roughness, warmth, and slipperiness*" in their own ways, and you can provide your baby with many board books and toys that have these different textures (Van de Rijt, Plooij, and Plas-Plooij 2019, 65).

Babies at this age who are exceptionally socially aware can see emotions in categories, as well. That is, they may put on an act and take advantage of your reactions by pretending to be sad, sweet, or distressed. This may seem like a manipulation, but they are simply experimenting with how they affect you and catching on to their ability to make you react. Don't take it personally. Instead, feel proud that your baby is so clever!

Transitional Objects

We all know about the Charles Schulz character Linus and his beloved blanket. He drags it around wherever he goes, nibbling on its corner or curling up with it when he needs even more security. Security objects such as blankets are part of the emotional support system that babies use in early years.

Your baby may choose a blanket, a soft toy, or even the satin trim on mommy's bathrobe as his transitional object. He'll probably make a choice between the ages of eight and twelve months and then keep that object with him for many years. When he's tired, it will help get him to sleep. When he's separated from you, it will be reassuring. When he's frightened or upset, it will comfort. If he's in a strange place, it will help him feel at home.

These are *not-me* objects that stand in for the mother and are called transitional objects because they help babies—and later children—make the emotional transition from dependence to independence. Transitional objects work because they feel soft, cuddly, and nice to touch. They are familiar and will carry your child's smell on them. This *lovey object* will remind your baby of the comfort and security of her own room and more—particularly, her own mother.

Despite myths to the contrary, transitional objects are never a signal to a baby's weakness or insecurity. In fact, they indicate the reverse: your baby is independently learning to regulate his need for soothing on his own. Transitional objects are so helpful that you may want to help your baby choose one and incorporate it into his nighttime ritual.

You can also make things easier for yourself by having two identical transitional security objects. Doing this allows you to wash one while the other is being dragged about, thus sparing your baby (and yourself) a potential emotional crisis and a worn lovey. If your baby chooses a large blanket, turn it into two by cutting it in half. She has little sense of size and won't notice. It's the feel and smell that she is looking for. If she's chosen a toy, try to find a duplicate as soon as possible. If you don't start rotating them early, your child may refuse the second one because it doesn't carry the smell and feel of the original one; she may experience it as unfamiliar and seek out the first one.

You may worry that your baby's transitional object promotes thumb-sucking with the item, and this may become true. But it's important to remember that thumb- or finger-sucking is a normal, natural way for a young one to self-regulate and soothe himself. He'll gradually give up both the transitional object and the sucking as he matures and finds other ways to cope with stress. (However, some teens still hold on to their original object in their rooms!)

The key to the importance of the transitional object is that it is a transition; instead of the mother regulating her infant's security, the baby learns to do so on her own. This is a milestone of great significance.

This ninth month will undoubtedly be full of fun and fascinating learning experiences—all through play. Remember that you and your baby are communicating all the time and that your baby is beginning to understand more and more of your intentions and feelings. Listen and learn as you solidify your emotional and loving relationship.

Month Nine Milestones

Before we discuss ideas for play, let's remember what a baby may be able to do at nine months old, according to Murkoff, Eisenberg, and Hathaway (2003, 416–417):

- seek a dropped object

- try and get a toy out of reach

- creep or crawl

- get into sitting position from tummy

- resist letting you take a toy away

- stand up when holding on to someone or something

- pick up tiny objects with thumb and finger

- say "mama" or "dada" without distinguishing to whom

- play peekaboo

- play patty-cake, clapping hands

- wave bye

- walk holding furniture (cruising)

- understand "no" but not obey

- roll a ball

- stand alone for a short time

- say a word

- respond to a one-step command with gestures, such as the parent saying "Give that to me" with her hand out and the baby responding in kind

Playtime Suggestions

Now let's take a look at what kind of play you can enjoy and expect from your nine-month-old.

- Your baby is ready to learn about the spaces around her. A large cardboard box can help her learn the concepts of "inside" and "outside," can provide a great place to hide during hide-and-seek games and can provide windows (if cut) for playing peekaboo.

- Your baby still enjoys things that are hidden. Now that he's so good at handling objects, he can enjoy new hunting and finding games. At a park or beach, show your baby a brightly colored baby safe object, like a rubber ball. (The brighter the better, because it's then easier to find.) Make sure your nine-month-old is looking and then dig in so the toy is under some sand. Then ask, "Where did it go?" Help put your baby's hand on the mound of sand until he finds it; then you can react with joy.

- Continue playing games like peekaboo and hide-and-seek; they help your baby continue to figure out the concept of object permanence (the idea that things exist even when you can't see them).

- Place objects around your baby that you know she'll recognize. Then ask, "Where's the spoon? the bunny . . . ?" Praise her when she gets it right and try again when she gets it wrong (all as you're still smiling, of course).

- Mirrors may become even more interesting to your baby at this age, as she is discovering that her reflection imitates her movements; your baby may even start babbling to the mirror. https://www.parents.com/advice/babies/baby development/how-should-i-play-with-a-9-month-old/

- Cause and effect games can still be a lot of fun. Your baby will love dropping, throwing, and banging just about anything to see what happens. Give your baby some plastic bowls or pots and pans, and he'll likely yelp with joy at the sounds he can make.

An Illustration of a Mother and Nine-Month-Old Baby at Play

Mommy: "Hi sweetie. Let's look at this big wall mirror together. See me pick you up high and low? See the baby in the mirror going up and down?"

The baby smiles and watches with fascination and glee, very attentive to the reflection.

Mommy: "Oh now let's move our heads up and down. See my head go up and down? See the baby's head go up and down? What fun we are having."

The baby eyes the mother's and baby's reflection with great curiosity and excitement.

A PLAY SESSION

Monday morning Caz and Semantha greet me at the door. Caz was away in Washington for the weekend and had only five hours sleep Sunday night. She leads me into the bedroom and closes the door. She places Semantha on the unmade bed amidst toys and blankets. Semantha is happy to be sitting in the middle of the toys and picks up different ones and rattles them or hits one against another. She smiles at me as she is doing this and keeps an eye on her mother who is straightening up the room.

Caz asks if I had a nice Mother's Day, and I say yes. She says for her Mother's Day Semantha got a lot of presents, but it was supposed to be a day for her (Caz)!

I ask her how Semantha reacted after she had been away for a few days, and she says first she turned away from her and then after a short while wanted to show her things. (Semantha stayed with close friends each night.) I pointed out, "Semantha's turning away was adjusting her feelings of loss and then when she was able to cope, she turned back, recognized you, and wanted to engage with you in play to reconnect. It shows that your bond is secure for her. Nice mothering!"

I try some joint play with Semantha sitting up where I show her to put a ball in a box. She does it, and we try a few successive times and sometimes she does it and other times not. She is happily playing. Sometimes she gets in the crawling position with one leg stuck underneath and then manages to sit up again.

I ask Caz how her mother is doing. She says she is home but the other day she drove herself to the emergency room without telling anyone because her hands and feet tingled from the medicine. Her thought processes still aren't exactly right, Caz says. She has a doctor's appointment on Tuesday for that.

Semantha plays for at least twenty minutes, smiling, mostly making sounds where her tongue comes out and she blows. Then she makes another sound which indicates to Caz that she is hungry. I notice that when Caz leaves the room to get the food, Semantha stops playing and calmly waits for her to return. She is too immersed in waiting for her mother to come back to continue playing and instead is watching the door.

When Caz returns, she mentions that Semantha didn't even know she was gone and I say, "That's not true. She watched the door waiting for your return the whole time. That's the *only* thing that was on her mind. She even stopped playing to just focus on waiting for you!"

Semantha eats happily opening her mouth wide for every spoonful. Once in a while she also makes that raspberry sound and Caz says, "no" to keep the food in her mouth. While it's understandable that Caz wants her baby to eat, I don't mention it for fear she might think I am critical, but she actually missed an opportunity for more communication vis-à-vis the raspberry sound which is intended to get her mother's attention. Still, Caz smiles at her even when she is generally quiet, thus, keeping up the interaction between mother and baby. A few times the food lands on the sheet which Caz quickly wipes up. After two containers Caz asks Semantha if she wants more. She finds out by putting the spoon to her mouth and Semantha opens her mouth for more. Again, mother and baby are communicating in this interactive way.

Caz leaves the room again to get more food and once again Semantha watches the door quietly waiting for her return. She ate most of the last container and indicates she is finished by not opening her mouth anymore. So, watching the door has a meaning and so does closing her mouth. Each action or gesture is intended to communicate. This is remarkable. I point out both almost missed events to Caz, so she can appreciate her baby is *intending* to communicate with her.

Caz lets her play a little more then says she needs a bath. Together we go into the bathroom. After Caz undresses Semantha on the changing table, she points out a small rash above the diaper line. Caz thinks it was from wearing clothes without a onesie underneath or it was the diaper, but she doesn't like the look of it and plans to show it to the doctor. I mention what an attentive mother she is.

In the bathroom, Caz fills the small tub with water and puts it in the large tub. Semantha splashes happily smiling with nonstop motion. She has a few little toys she plays with but mostly enjoyed splashing. After a while of letting her splash about, Caz washes her and pours water over her head which Semantha tolerates very well, being quite used to it. After the washing she plays some more and then is wrapped warmly in a big towel and taken back to the bedroom and put on the changing table. I mention to Caz that all of these interactions are so lovely and motherly, and she can trust that her baby feels their closeness.

When I note that Semantha is nonstop motion on the changing table reaching for everything she can manage, Caz says, "Oh, so much energy!" Then she dresses her, and Semantha calms down and lets her mother dress her fairly easily though she is uncomfortable when clothes go over her head. Caz says, "I've never seen anyone hate getting dressed so much."

I respond, "I don't think it's not liking dressing exactly, but when something is put over her head, she loses her opportunity to see what's going on. She's not objecting to the clothes but to the lost opportunity to understand what's going on around her." Caz is pleased to understand that difference and appreciates her daughter's interest in her surroundings.

Semantha is then put on the bed to play some more with Caz and me. Semantha reaches for my beads and Caz says, "No," but I say, "I don't mind. Let her play with them. She's just connecting with me in this way." Then I take them off and give them to her and Caz guesses she likes them on my neck better, which may have been accurate because that meant she is not only interested in the beads but in my wearing them, that is, our connection and interaction. She plays with them for quite a while. Then it is time to go and Caz says they'll walk me to the door. I try waving bye-bye to Semantha but she is not ready to understand that gesture yet. Caz and I wish each other a good week.

What Does Caz Learn from Playing with Semantha?

Caz has become very adept at following her baby's communications. She, however, didn't realize how intently Semantha was watching and waiting for her when she went out of the room. This is a very important milestone for Caz to be aware of. Semantha is now able to recognize not only object permanence (objects reappear after they disappear) but is also working on object constancy (important people reappear after they disappear) which will continue to improve as she gets older.

$\sim$

You might notice how this baby was learning to tolerate her mother's absence at times. Naturally in daily life this will occur sometimes for moments, while other times it may have to be for a few days. Find out how your baby is coping when you aren't present. If you are gone for a day or more, it's to be expected that your baby will need time to adjust first to being cared for by, hopefully, well-known others and then be able to remember you are number one and have returned. Although perhaps she'll be initially upset when she sees you, in time she will become glad to see you again. If your relationship is secure, she will try to engage you in play just as you saw with Caz and Semantha.

If your baby doesn't engage in play quickly, you can gently take the initiative to talk to her, so she remembers your voice and touch her gently, so she remembers your touch and smell and then begin to play with a favorite familiar toy if she is interested. Follow your baby's pace. Each mother-baby pair have their own relationship, and it takes some babies longer than others to readjust after being separated from their mother.

Emotional Attunement with Your Baby

What Do Researchers Have to Say about Your Ten-Month-Old?

What are the acts and processes that let other people know that you are feeling something very like what they are feeling? How can you get "inside of" other people's subjective experience and then let them know that you have arrived there, without using words? (Stern 1985, 138)

Infants are only about ten or more months old when they are beginning this learning process about other's feelings.

We know that a mother and her baby imitate each other, but this doesn't mean that either understands the *feeling state* behind the other's actions. Feeling state refers to the physiological experience that comes with a feeling. Mother and baby might not have similar inner experiences of feeling states, even when their actions are the same. For example, you may smile even if you are feeling sad inside. If the infant vocalizes, his mother vocalizes back in return; if the baby makes a face, his mother responds with a similar face. But, beginning at nine months, mothers seem to intuitively know that they can go beyond exact imitation in order to match the feeling states of their babies. Stern calls this *affect attunement* (140). In other words, when a mother recognizes the inner state of feelings between her and her baby, she is in tune with her infant. Understanding these inner feelings goes beyond just trying to match or imitate a baby's facial expression.

Affect Attunement and Play

Imagine a child fitting a puzzle piece in the right place. Her mother gleefully exclaims, "YES, thatta girl!" She doesn't say, "Yes, thatta girl," but intuitively matches her emphasis to the task her baby has accomplished. This is attunement, and it is very exciting because the quality of the relationship between mother and child is so significant (Stern 1985, 141). The mother's stated response, "Thatta girl," reflects the inner *feeling state* that she intuits from the child's physical action of putting in the puzzle piece. The intensity level of the mother's words and the duration of her voice is matched by her body movements. In other words, the feeling state—not the action—is being matched.

The idea that the mother and baby can share same or somewhat different feelings about an action is more significant to their relationship than just the behavior itself.

Affect attunement occurs, then, when behaviors express a feeling. So now when a mother or baby imitates the other, they may do so without imitating the other's exact behavioral expression (142). *These attunements shift the focus from the behavior to the feeling behind the behavior.* Attunement is more implicitly accomplished than empathy, which is consciously done. In fact, attunement is almost automatic or almost outside of awareness.

An experiment concerning attunement might help to further explain the concept. In the study, mothers played with their babies for ten to fifteen minutes and were videoed while doing so. The experimenters then replayed the videos for the mothers and asked them nonjudgmental questions to ascertain what had happened. The experimenters stopped the video when the baby made an affective expression such as a facial, vocal, gestural, or postural reaction—that was followed by the mother's responding in an observable way. It was evident from this study that the babies had seen, heard, or felt these responses from their mothers. The babies were eight to twelve months old.

The experimenters called these events (affective expressions followed by a response) *interpersonal communion* (148), because the mothers indicated they were trying "to be with," "to share," "to participate in," and "to join" their babies when they responded.

The mothers also indicated that they responded at a level of intensity that matched what they saw in their babies (148). "Communion means to share in another's experience with no attempt to change what that person is doing or believing" (148). In the experiment, the babies did not react to their mothers' responses when the responses were appropriately matched. However, if the mother over or underplayed the event in her reaction, the baby would stop as if to inquire what was happening.

That's how the experimenters differentiated actual attunements from purposeful mis-attunements. Most often, actual attunements happened when the mother's actions or vocalizations matched the intensity of her baby's actions in play.

A mother can find this attunement through the close timing of simple tasks during play, such as when her baby reaches for a toy, holds a block, kicks a foot, or listens to a sound. Simply put, if you can catch on to your baby's feelings, your baby feels *with* you, and there is communion.

Infant Development

Let's step back a moment to question what your ten-month-old baby may be doing, so that we know what affective experiences can be expected.

Your baby should be able to:

- stand while holding something or someone

- pull up to standing from sitting

- resist if you attempt to take toy away

- say "dada" or "mama" without distinguishing who

And may be able to:

- relish peekaboo

- show back-and-forth gestures

- sit after lying on tummy

- clap hands

- wave bye

- pick small objects up with thumb and forefinger

- walk while holding on to sofa

- understand but not obey

- momentarily stand alone

- point to something

- roll a ball

- drink from a cup

- stand alone

- use sounds as if speaking in a made-up language

- say another word in addition to "mama" or "dada"

- respond to a singular request with gestures, like putting their hand out when hearing "Give that to me."

- walk. (Murkoff, Eisenberg, and Hathaway 2003, 435–436)

Playtime Suggestions

At ten months old, babies may invent a game by accident. For example, a baby may crawl, race, and get ahead of herself then become tangled in her limbs and flop on her face. When the mother spontaneously laughs, she is reinforcing these actions. The baby then does it all on purpose to get mommy's laugh again, and a new game has begun; the mother has inadvertently turned what could have become a fear into a positive experience

(Brazelton 1969, 223). This can happen in many different forms and is another great example of your baby's ability to have fun with cause and effect.

However, babies at this age can be self-conscious and suspicious of others' motives. For example, Brazelton tells of a baby who was moving and humming to music until he noticed he was being observed. Then he stopped to make sure he wasn't being laughed *at*, still unsure of his experimentation with his voice (24).

Another instance of a baby turning his curiosities into games was when a ten-month-old crawled near the stove and heard his mother's "No." The baby paused to make sure his mother was watching him and then crawled closer to the stove, waiting for the naysaying again. He turned this into a repetitive game until his mother ignored him (29).

Another baby created a game with language. Whenever she learned a new word, she would repeat it to herself during play—without regard to its meaning. Talking itself became the game. However, she had a mind of her own. When her parents pushed her to use her newfound language and say "Bye-bye," the baby refused to say it (231).

As the parent, you can instigate games for your baby as well. Teach her the different parts of a doll by pointing to the doll's hair, eyes, ears, and toes and naming the parts aloud. Once your baby learns the words on the doll, she can point to herself when the parts are named. For example, you can ask, "Where are Laura's eyes?" and Laura can make the connection with herself, pointing to her own eyes.

Ten months is also a great time to play games that capitalize on your baby's new motor skills—especially her pincer grasp (when she grabs tiny objects between her thumb and pointer finger). Give her a bucket full of toys and let her dump it out and fill it up again. You can also give her stacking toys, like rings and cups. Be aware that she may want to play with them separately before she begins stacking them.

You can also continue singing songs that encourage finger games, improving his fine motor skills, and that have a lot of repetition, like the "Wheels on the Bus." Although he can't sing along, he enjoys their repetition and will pick up a few words now and then.

Here are more simple games you can play with your ten-month-old.

- Show your baby how to push a small car or truck along the floor. After a while, he'll learn to let go so that the car rolls by itself.

- Play follow-the-leader. He'll love to imitate. Use simple gestures like tapping the table, opening and closing your fist, or putting a hat on your head. Narrate what you're doing, so he can learn the words as he mimics your actions.

- Talk to him on a real or play phone. He'll learn the fun of carrying on a conversation.

- Go outside. At this stage, he'll enjoy putting things into other things, so he'll enjoy putting leaves, twigs, or toys in a pail.

- Put a small toy inside a paper bag or box. As he struggles to get it, he'll increase his understanding of *inside and outside*.

- Build her a tower of blocks. She will enjoy watching them as they fall apart and even fall, and she may try to build something herself.

- Reserve a cabinet for your baby's toys; putting them away can be a game in itself, because she's putting things into a special place.

- Help her blow bubbles using a straw in her bathwater. You blow first and then see if she'll imitate you.

- Hide a toy in a box or bag and suggest that your baby get it for you.

- Show your baby how to balance blocks and build them into a column. Then give the tower a gentle push and watch them tumble.

- Clap with sticks and spoons and other utensils.

These next few ideas come from occupational therapist Urszula Semerda of SensoryLifestyle.com, and provide a variety of ways to encourage your baby to explore their ever-expanding environment.

- Play in a bathtub or wading pool.

- Play with cooked noodles, or any food! Don't be afraid of a mess.

- Create obstacle courses with tents and tunnels made from pillows. Join in the climbing and crawling.

- Play with balloons. Let them bounce off baby's hands and head. As always, watch your baby carefully and remove any pieces that may pop.

- Pull your baby across the floor on a soft blanket.

- Run slowly from one side of the sofa to the other, encouraging your baby to cruise back and forth.

At this age there are so many fun games and activities to engage with your baby. See the Additional Resources section for more ideas.

- https://howtoadult.com/play-with-10-6471.html/

- https://www.greatdad.com/baby/how-to-play-with-your-tcn-month-old-baby/

  https://www.parents.com/advice/babies/baby-development/how-should-i-play-with-a-10-month-old/

Remember that all of these games are combined with the *attuned feeling states* between mother or father and baby, which makes them all so shareable and enjoyable. The shared feeling states we call attunement are as important or even more important than the achievement of these tasks, because they have to do with the ever-growing relationship between parent and baby.

An Illustration of a Father and Ten-Month-Old Baby at Play

Daddy decided to make up a story about himself and his baby. He narrated their whole day from the time the baby awoke, was fed, was changed, played, took a nap, and played some more until the next meal. The baby listened attentively staring at his father's facial expressions and lip movements. The baby's comprehension exceeded his language, and the father knew to speak slowly, so his baby could catch on.

Then Daddy drew pictures of all the events of the day and narrated the events again pointing to his pictures. The baby was fascinated mostly because he knew his father was fascinated. This wasn't only about language, identification of pictures, and narration of events, all of which were very important, but about the affective interchange between this devoted loving father and his baby.

A PLAY SESSION

I hadn't seen Caz and Semantha for three weeks. The first missed week I got a call from Caz indicating that Semantha was in the hospital for the whole weekend. She had trouble breathing and was grunting. Mark, who is an EMT, was over and recognized right away something was wrong. So, they brought her to the hospital to find out she had a high white blood count and viral pneumonia. She went in on a Friday and stayed through Sunday.

When I reached Caz directly, she told me that she stayed the whole time in the hospital by her side with Mark. By Sunday her lungs were clear. Caz's reaction to taking her baby to the hospital was, "I couldn't believe I was admitting her!"

Semantha, Caz, and I meet next at Caz's mother's home. Semantha begins to play with the top of a pot, quite actively banging it on the wooden floor and mouthing it. Caz tells me she doesn't worry when things go in her mouth. Babies even adjust to sand in their mouths and she isn't overprotective that way.

She also tells me she saw Semantha pulling at her ear one day and went to the doctor who said she's teething, which was the first time she'd had any reaction to all the teething. Caz tells me that Semantha said "Dada" only when Mark was around and "Bah Bah" when her brother was around. But she still did not ever say "Ma Ma." I say that doesn't reflect her feelings for her as her mother. It is just the specific consonants she is capable of saying at this time. Caz is relieved.

Semantha seems to amuse herself a great deal with a pot lid and when it slips a distance away, she gets into a crawling position and then as soon as she looks like she will crawl, she slumps on her tummy. This happens several times.

A few more times, Semantha looks like she was about to crawl and the grandmother comes in at one moment and says she can just feel she is so ready. I agree.

Then instead of moving forward to get the top she starts sliding backward which is unintended and frustrating. Caz puts her in a sitting position again, and she is happy once more. Several times as she reaches and retrieves the top, I comment, "She really thinks about what she wants now and goes to get it. This is wonderful intentional behavior. Yay for Semantha!"

Caz says Semantha is waving bye-bye and saying "wow." But she can't get her to say it then. She also confides in me, "I feel that when Semantha is away from me, she doesn't miss me."

I say, "I'm sure that isn't true," and ask, "How does she react when you pick her up at day care?"

Caz says, "Semantha is all smiles. Also, when I leave her at day care she never cries. She is fine and very comfortable there."

I say, "It sounds like she has adjusted well to being apart from you because you have helped her become a secure baby. That hardly means she doesn't miss you. It means she, in fact, trusts you'll return, and that is why she greets you with a smile."

Eventually Semantha shows some signs of frustration, making quiet but complaining type sounds, and Caz decides she is hungry. She picks her up and comments that she doesn't like to cuddle.

I ask, "What do you make of that? Do you miss her more baby side when she used to cuddle closely?"

Caz gives it thought and says, "I guess it's hard to adjust to her becoming more independent. Yes. I think you're right."

What Does Caz Learn from Playing with Semantha?

Most poignant in this visit was that it was very important for Caz to reconnect with me after the scary experience of Semantha being in the hospital. Caz needed a lot of mothering herself after the traumatic experience of her baby being sick. Mark was an excellent supporter, but no one could take away all she'd been through with her baby. She clearly needed my attentive support.

~

Unexpected and uncertain situations, like a baby's sickness that is severe enough to bring her to a hospital, are difficult experiences for parents even when your baby is well cared for. The fear of what could occur may be on your mind. It's important to have another adult to support you on the phone or better yet, in person. Feelings of uncertainty about your baby's health and well-being are trying and sometimes traumatic. Expect you will need time to recover from such a situation and need loving support from others as you give your loving attention to your baby.

Imagining Stories with Your Baby

What Do the Researchers Have to Say about Your Eleven-Month-Old?

During this next month of your baby's life, researchers suggest to continue all the play suggestions listed in the previous chapter, but expect your baby's abilities to be refined even more.

You can also start story-making with your now inventive child. She may play with dolls, trucks, and other toys that require some imagination—and you can join her! Play with her trucks as she makes them go on trips, and her dolls as she tucks them in or puts their heads on a pillow.

You may also notice her play seems more purposeful than usual as she takes a plastic hammer and pounds pegs into a hole. Don't forget to narrate this play, as it will increase her language and help you both to enjoy your time together. You can add new elements to her simple stories, experimenting with whether she will go along with your new perspective or train of thought. Now that your baby's imagination is starting to bloom, play can take on a whole new level of fun, excitement, and wonder.

Infant Development

Remember that your eleven-month-old is becoming a toddler or wanderer. He is (or will be soon) cruising about, holding on to furniture or your hands. He may even let go and try walking on his own—so prepare yourself for more independence. Some babies first try to stand on their toes or on one leg. Encourage this activity but be there for his falls. In fact, he may begin to be clingy again after trying these upright activities; respond to his needs for refueling with extra hugs!

Some mighty, adventurous toddlers choose climbing as a way to discover and explore. They'll climb over their crib railings and may get in a few precarious situations—so watch out. Your baby will also like opening and closing cabinet drawers around this age, so be sure to lock up any chemicals or cleaning tools that she can get her deft and curious hands on.

As your baby's hand-eye coordination improves, he'll also enjoy learning how things work. He may find it fun to arrange toys by size and color as well as take them apart and put them back together. Stacking blocks and nesting cups are excellent toys for these baby quests (https://www.webmd.com/parenting/baby/baby-development-11-month-old).

Play Suggestions

- Show your baby how bits of food or pieces of paper can be made into a face on her plate.

- Show your baby how to jump on a mattress like a trampoline.

- Make tunnels out of pillows or cardboard boxes for toys to go through, and then encourage your baby to wiggle through!

- Have two adults lie on the floor with a space between them and encourage your happy baby to crawl back and forth over their backs.

- Fill a plastic container with water and show your baby how to paint; don't worry if the water goes on the floor!

- Play in and with sand.

- Match, sort, and group toys by color or shape as you play together to see if your baby understands the idea of categories (this may be a bit too soon for most babies).

- Stand your baby on his knees or feet and rock slowly to music together.

- Watch your baby repeat new skills again and again, like stacking blocks or taking things out of a bag and putting them back in again.

- Take turns doing things.

- Try making funny faces and see if your baby imitates them or reacts.

- Clap hands—both your own and your babies'. She will love watching, imitating, and playing new clapping games.

- Encourage your baby to help you do housework, like doing the dishes or wiping the floor.

- Experiment with the sounds that different objects make around the house, like a wooden or metal ball, a spoon, or a spatula.

- Ask your baby to go and get simple objects for you to use by naming them. (Easy Baby Life; New Kids Center)

With all these fun and interesting activities, remember once again that your baby cares that you know how she feels. Stay attuned to her moods and temperamental changes and voice her feelings as you understand them in words (like sad, mad, and glad). She'll gradually pick up on some of these words as you further develop your relationship. Yes! You have been building a relationship all these months. To highlight this connection, you can even tell her stories about what the two of you are doing each day. Your baby knows she can count on you and trust you.

An Illustration of a Mother and Eleven-Month-Old Baby at Play

Mommy is very interested in her baby's ability to stack cups and watch them fall down. This intrigues her not because of the motor development but because of the emotional experience she and her baby feel together as they play. The baby regularly checks her mother's face to see her reaction. If the mother laughs, the baby laughs. If the mother patiently waits with a more composed expression, she notices her baby is more somber, too. This mother is more interested in being attuned to her baby's feelings than the actual activities which are so numerous at this time.

When the baby is cruising on the living room couch, she looks back at her mother to see how she is reacting. Her mother smiles, and so she knows it is safe to continue on her venture. This "social referencing" isn't missed at all by this attuned mother who appreciates her daughter's wish for her mother's protection and approval.

A PLAY SESSION

Semantha is in Caz's arms when they greet me at the door. Semantha's eyes look a little glassy like she might be sick. Caz takes her right to the floor, so she can show me what Semantha's learned. Semantha is interested in saying sounds to me. Caz says, "She's infatuated with you. We haven't been here for days. We've been at Mark's."

Then, Semantha, who seems to have a larger sound vocabulary gets on her knees at a low table and then stands up on one leg, the other is bent, then eventually she stands and holds on to the table. I say, "Ooh, she's standing. That is a new development!"

Caz looks delighted. But she says she hopes she doesn't walk before they go on their plane ride. I say laughing, "You'll be running up and down the aisles."

Semantha sits and stands and crawls a bit. Caz says she's very independent. "She doesn't need me."

I respond, "She is independent, but she needs you—maybe more than ever as she experiments with getting around on her own. Believe me, she still wants to know where you are."

Caz agrees and gives her a hug and some kisses. She says she can play on her own as long as I'm here. Again, Caz's attachment to me is so meaningful to her, especially as she transitions to her baby's new independence.

Caz feels Semantha's forehead and thinks she feels warm. She tells me, "She's been sick so often, and she threw up at day care. I wonder what she ate, because she is allergic to a lot of foods, but she's not a thrower upper." She adds the doctor said the problem is with her adenoids. That's why she's been getting sick so often. Then Caz decides to take her temperature.

I comment, "It's so hard when Semantha isn't well. But your nurturing attention is just what she needs. You are a very responsible mother taking her to her physician and coping with her medical needs. It's hard, but you are doing a wonderful, loving job."

We go in the bedroom and she lays Semantha on the changing table, takes her temperature, and finds it is 102 degrees. She gives her the little bit of Motrin she has left, and Semantha lets some slip out of her mouth. She then decides to feed her and give her a cool bath to bring her temperature down.

Caz is getting the food ready just as Semantha is calling "Ma Ma" over and over. Caz says, "I know this is your way of communicating with me; you are hungry."

I comment how well Caz understands Semantha's intentions. Then, when Semantha calls out very loudly and repeatedly, Caz tells her she can't yell to get what she wants. She gives her some finger foods to eat while she's waiting. I comment how well she has managed this situation with her hungry baby and finger foods were just the right thing to do.

She starts to feed Semantha who has a few spoonfuls but is more interested in her finger foods. So, Caz lets her finish those first. She sits there a little while longer saying different sounds and waving to me. I wave back.

Caz takes her out of the highchair and brings her into the bedroom to get her ready for the bath. On the changing table she reaches for a plastic bag and Caz takes the bag away and gives her something else to hold. She says, "Semantha had a great time at Mark's, because she could cruise around and liked all the hardwood floors to crawl on."

Caz chooses a towel, gets the bath ready, and puts her in. Semantha loves it and is very happy now. She tries to crawl and stand up and Caz says to sit down, and she does. She plays with a Winnie the Pooh character in the tub, dropping it in the water and then reaching for it over and over. Then Caz comments on what little she needs to have a good time. Caz feels her forehead, and she feels cooler. She says it's time to get out. She picks her up and brings her into the bedroom and puts her on the changing table. She puts lotion all over her and suctions her nose.

I comment, "Semantha is really very patient, and you take such good care of her when she isn't feeling well."

It's time for me to go. Caz reiterates that she'll see me next week. She comments it's amazing how long I've known them. She says, as if she and Semantha are both speaking, "Bye-bye, Dr. Hollman. Drive safe." It's a moving emotional moment for Caz to see me leave especially on a day when she needs extra support because Semantha isn't feeling well.

What Did Caz Learn from Playing with Semantha?

As my time with Caz and Semantha at her home is drawing to a close, Caz is revealing the attachment she feels with me and comments openly on how long we've known each other. It's important that I'm very attuned to these feelings toward me. I've been the one constant in her life with Semantha for a year as many tumultuous things have happened such as her mother's mental illness, her new devoted love with Mark, and of course all Semantha's vast growth and development. Remembering how Caz is a very young mother with little consistent maternal support, I understand just as Semantha needs Caz's attention and approval for trust and safety, Caz also needs the same from me.

Semantha has developed well during this first year trusting her mother, tolerating well her short absences with joyful reunions, enjoying playing with other children at day care, and reaching all milestones on time. She has developed a *core self* that is joyful and attained a positive secure attachment with her mother.

———

As shown with Caz and Semantha, just as your baby needs your trust and attention, you, too, need consistent, caring support. This may come from a spouse, a parent, a trusted friend, or a therapist. This supportive person will naturally become very important to you especially if you are a new mother. Be kind to yourself and accept that you have needs as well as your baby.

Learning about Cause *and* Effect *with* Your Baby

What Do Researchers Have to Say about Your Twelve-Month-Old?

Can you believe your baby is twelve months old—a one-year-old? As you've noticed, your baby is growing more sophisticated daily. At twelve months old, she can understand not only *general* cause and effect but also the differences between *physical* and *psychological* cause and effect.

For example, remember the experiment from the chapter on the third month when babies made a mobile move with a string tied to their toes? If the ribbon was taken away, they still kicked—as if the connection were there—until the novelty wore off. Some babies also thought that if they cooed and smiled, the mobile would move, because mommy always reacts to coos and smiles.

Now at one year, your baby better understands how events and objects influence each other. Babies know right away, for example, that they can pull a cloth with a toy on top of it toward them, bringing them the toy. Even further, they understand that if the cloth is *next* to an object but not under it, nothing will happen. Your baby didn't realize this months ago (Gopnik, Meltzoff, and Kuhl 1999, 76–77)!

If you tried the mobile experiment months ago, try it again and see how your baby's mind has expanded into new territory. Your baby is pre-programmed to want to know how things work in general and in a causal way. That's why a busy box toy (a plastic activity board for hands-on, fine-motor-skill building that has noise-making buttons and various gadgets to manipulate) is a good one to have on hand, because babies vary the actions they perform on objects now.

You can (and should!) do fun experiments to help your baby explore the world and its many intricacies. For example, give her a new toy car and let her discover what she can do with it. Who knows how she will experiment and explore with it! Perhaps show her that by tapping the car on the ground it will make a different noise than when you tap it on a quilt (88). Or maybe she will discover this on her own!

As an even simpler experiment, put your baby in a new room that she hasn't explored before and watch her take off to discover its mysteries. Your baby is increasingly observant, and this twelfth month can be just as exciting for you to watch as it is for her to explore.

Infant Development

Language

Your newborn, who could only discriminate between the sounds of different languages, is now busy grouping the sounds he hears into categories of the particular language(s) used in his culture. "By one year of age, babies' speech categories begin to resemble those of the adults in their culture" (Gopnik, Meltzoff, and Kuhl 1999, 108).

Actually "at six months this process has already begun and the six- to twelve-month time span is the critical time for sound organization" (108). Babies are sorting out sounds according to the sounds they hear every day, and that's what they end up sticking to; they filter out what is typical for the language they hear.

In other words, they actually master sounds first and then form words. It is about at one year that words, in fact, are heard. By nine months babies learn that certain words are stressed in certain syllables—such as BASEball or POPcorn—and which sound combinations are used in their own language. As you've been playing and talking for this past year, you have been giving your baby invaluable information that will help him form words.

By seven or eight months, you may remember how he began to babble vowel syllables such as "dada" or "baba." This milestone marked the end of a broad understanding of universal language sounds as he began to discriminate which sounds fit the language he heard around him (113). Much later, around eighteen months, your baby will discover more often how specific words have meanings, but for now he is putting together sounds—learning to understand a few words and directions and having fun doing so (125).

The Wish for Independence

One-year-old babies continue the many activities they have been trying for the last two months. However, there may be an additional desire for independence now that they are walking or trying to walk. According to Brazelton (2006), this wish for independence can make your baby more self-conscious, as they don't want to feel invaded.

This means that you shouldn't pressure your baby with intense, prodding stares. Your baby may also show a new irritability, a wish to make her own decisions, and efforts to do everything on her own. Brazelton calls this a *touchpoint* because of its significance in development. In fact, your baby may say "All by myself" over and over as soon as she can speak. In all of this, she is just testing your limits repeatedly and asserting herself—which admittedly can be much more difficult to manage yet exciting all at the same time.

Remember that your little one cares about herself and her ability to affect others. As she is learning what she can and cannot do with her body as well as with words and gestures, she is soaking in information about how the world responds. With the ability to stand and maybe walk, she experiences the effects of gravity. When her ambitions and her growing abilities are not always in perfect harmony, you may find yourself dealing with some outbursts. Consider this behavior a form of communication for you to unravel, not something to worry about. Your baby is learning to express herself and even protest sometimes. It's great that she has her sense of agency and can speak her mind in her own way. If we listen and understand and don't overreact, she will feel accepted as the unique individual that she is, and you will enjoy each other.

Now or very soon, your baby has somehow become a toddler! This brings new ambivalence to her abilities. Does she want to walk away on her own or retreat and find you? She considers, "Do I want to do it my mommy's way or my own way? Will I or won't I? Do I or don't I?"

These are persistent questions that will be evident in her back-and-forth behavior, giving you a view of her *inner* struggles. All of this is a close interweaving of motor and emotional development. Standing and walking become her first priority—even when she's happily eating at her highchair. Suddenly, she may try to rise up and get out, leaving you to wonder what just happened! You may even start to play games of diapering her while she's standing up, because lying down is too frustrating for her (Brazelton 2006, 135–137).

Learning

Pointing and gesturing will become increasingly specific, and your toddler will combine these with his eye and facial gestures to explain his world. If he wants to get—or keep—your attention, you may see him point and say a word. If the word isn't clear, you can try to clarify it, helping your baby continue to learn his words! In this fashion, names get connected with the right people and things.

Object Permanence

Your toddler will still love testing object permanence, especially because she can go greater distances now. When she goes around a corner, she may look (or at least call) to see if you have objects that were just there. While she had no separation anxiety just a little while ago, he may now protest and worry. *This is progress, not regression.*

Rest assured, she understands object permanence, but you are not an inanimate object that may be hidden and then reappear. You are the *person* who makes her feel secure. As she is more mobile, it may become more difficult for her to be separate from you. Not until around the three-year mark will she be able, over many months, to master *object constancy*. This refers to knowing that when *people* are out of sight, they have not disappeared forever but can return. At this point, your baby can leave you, but understanding the reverse—you leaving her—will not come easily. Thus, games of peekaboo and saying "bye-bye" take on new dimensions of importance now and in the future.

Motor Skills: Using Two Hands at Once

Another fun development your baby may display at this age is the desire to hold objects in both hands. When you offer a third object to him while he plays, he will become hesitant to give up one of the first two and may try to hold all three. This may lead him to hold two small objects in one hand and another under his arm—or to discover that he can hold one object in his mouth! This all becomes a game of reaching and retrieval; your little one is becoming an astute problem solver.

Causality

Causality is also prominent. You can help your baby to learn this by showing him cause-and-effect with his toys. For example, let him watch you push a wind-up car and make it move. He'll probably want to do it himself and may or may not be able to manage it! Busy boxes are great for exploring cause and effect as well.

Playtime Suggestions

- Your baby may be cruising and getting ready for those first steps, and her balance has likely gotten better. Cruise along with her, singing happily to make her smile.

- Block building is another fun game. Stack blocks on top of each other until they fall. She may feel frustrated, but let her learn and try again.

- Your baby understands a lot of what you say. Continue talking and singing to her to your heart's delight.

- Now's a great time to play games that will increase her motor skills—especially her pincer grasp (the ability to grab small objects between thumb and pointer finger). Bring out the Cheerios or colored dowels that can easily be picked up in a pincer grasp.

- Your baby loves to drop and throw things, so give him a pail filled with objects and see what he does with them.

- Try stacking objects, though he may first prefer to play with them one by one.

- Encourage fine motor development with finger games and songs like "Itsy-Bitsy Spider" and "Five Little Ducks." Although babies this age can't sing yet, they love to follow with their hands and will continue to enjoy the sounds of melody and words.

- By the time of her first birthday, your baby will enjoy imitative play and love following your lead with plastic phones, kitchen utensils, tools, dolls, cars, and animals.

- Your baby may enjoy purposeful play, like using a plastic hammer to pound pegs into a hole or finding a pillow to prop up a doll's head.

- Whatever the play, it's important that you join in since he'll learn much more from watching you than anything else (Halpern 2015, "How Should I Play with a 12-Month-Old?").

- Now is the time to see what interests your baby has when left to her own devices. Take her to different environments—like new rooms, the park, and the ocean—and see what she enjoys doing.

- Point and name different objects and see if she tries to reach for or name them.

- Give her a cup of water and see what she does with it (under your watchful eyes).

- Sway and dance to different tunes and see what music your baby seems to prefer.

- Get easy-to-hold board books and cloth books and continue reading.

- Make different animal noises as you point to the animals in picture books and with toy animal figures. He'll soon catch on to the differences and maybe imitate a few—if he hasn't already!

- Do everyday routines, like brushing your hair, and see if he wants to try and brush your hair too—or even his own.

- Play with a flashlight, showing him shadows and blinking lights in a darkened room. Also get stickers that glow in the dark, which can make your baby smile with delight (Halpern 2015; wikiHow).

- Put circular objects like beads or cereal on a string and see if your baby catches on using her pincer grasp.

- Wrap up some of her toys and have her unwrap them like make-believe presents. The unwrapping is the fun.

- Gather up your different sized plastic containers and watch her put them inside each other or stack them on top of each other.

- Give your toddler a little massage while she's lying down, sitting on your lap, or even standing up. Rub your toddler's legs and feet, moving in a downward motion. Then do the same thing with her arms and hands. Don't forget her fingers (try to gently open her fists if she's clenching them). You can even play gentle music at the same time. This can help your little one to calm down before or after a nap (Baby Centre UK).

- Show your baby a mirror and test whether or not she thinks her reflection is another baby or herself: first, show her herself in the mirror, and then put lipstick on her nose. If she touches the baby's nose in the mirror, she does not know it's herself. If she touches her own nose; she recognizes herself. This usually happens between twelve and fifteen months. What does your baby do?

Congratulations, you've made it through the first twelve months—with a lot of play and conversing. You've learned to share affective moments, challenged your baby's knowledge of cause and effect, and, of course, built a special bond. Your relationship is wondrous, as your baby trusts you to help him, limit him, teach him, hug him, and love him in all your individual, endearing ways! As you continue to build your trusting relationship, remember that affective sharing, that wonderful sharing of emotions, is as important or more important than his achievements.

An Illustration of a Mother and Twelve-Month-Old Baby at Play

Mother notices that nap times are getting shorter and nighttime sleeping is getting longer. So new routines or rituals for nighttime sleep are on Mommy's mind. She learns about gentle massage, an innovative way to gently soothe your baby and secure your relationship in a physical way even more.

So, Mommy lays her baby in the crib and gently caresses the top of her head, her shoulders, her arms, hands, and fingers, and then proceeds to slowly circle her fingers on the baby's tummy and down her legs and feet and toes. The mother may hum quietly as she does this. Daddy joins in massaging baby's other foot. The baby clearly releases tension and relaxes enjoying the gentle, soft, soothing touch. Before Mommy and Daddy even notice, baby's eyes are closing, and she is drifting into her nighttime long sleep. How soothing this is for mother, father, and baby.

A PLAY SESSION

When Caz and Semantha arrive for our first visit in my office, I invite them in from the waiting room. Caz sits on the couch and puts Semantha on the floor. She tells me that Semantha just got a haircut.

I reply, "She looks really cute. She does look a little different."

Caz says, "She looks older."

Caz and I get on the floor with toys she brought. She has two blocks with different textures on each side and they fit together. Semantha bangs them together as she continues to look around. Then Caz takes out another toy, a rattle, and Semantha tries that.

Semantha puts out her hand to me, and I tap it with my hand. Caz says, "C'mon Semantha, do high five," and they do it with their hands. Semantha crawls a bit and a shoe comes off. Caz says. "That's what she's been trying to do. She doesn't like to wear shoes."

I say, "She likes the feel of her bare little toes."

Semantha is talking a lot with various sounds strung together in a conversational way.

After playing for a while with the toys Caz brought, she begins to adventure around crawling in the direction of some toys I have in a corner. She goes part of the way and then goes to Caz's lap. I comment, "It seemed too far, so she had to check back with you." Caz is very welcoming and gives her a nice hug and kiss and Semantha folds into her body gladly. Then Caz lays her on her back on the floor and kisses her tummy and face and Semantha laughs a hearty laugh. This continues a few times. Then Semantha goes back to exploring. She needed what is called *refueling* with her mother before going back to play.

She gets herself to the toys and touches a large stuffed animal dog that's actually a puppet. She shrinks back from it as if it is real. Caz says intuitively, "She doesn't know if it's real or not." Then she stays away from it and explores in another direction finding a chair at a table that she can hold on to and stand up. Watching her explore this new environment in her own way is delightful for Caz and for me.

Semantha is the one doing all the talking. When she looks at me and talks, I imitate the sound in response. She crawls back to the toys and is less afraid of the dog puppet now. She touches it carefully, stops, then starts again, touching it until she's more comfortable.

Caz makes it move, and Semantha is uncertain about it but intrigued.

Semantha finds a spoon and a pot with blocks in it. She takes the blocks and bangs them together. Caz says how independent Semantha is. She's checking with her now, making frequent eye contact as she plays, but at Mark's and her mother's, she just goes all around on her own. By this time, both her shoes are off her feet, and she's rubbing her feet on the carpet trying to get her socks off.

Semantha is really intrigued by the dog stuffed animal/puppet and is now touching it and backing away and touching it again over and over. Then she picks it up and holds it, feeling less scared. Caz says she's never seen her be so interested in something before. Then Caz realizes it's a puppet and puts her hand in it. Caz starts to make it move, and then it dawns on her that it might seem too real, so she stops. Semantha plays with it some more.

Then she leaves it and goes back to investigate what is in her mother's bag and pulls out a diaper. Caz says, "Why do you need the diaper to play with?" I suggest she's finding something already very familiar. Then, she plays with the blocks her mother brought. She plays a game with me giving me a block and then I give it back; we do this a few times. I notice when I point to something, she understands the gesture very well.

At some point she climbs onto my lap on the floor like she does with Caz. I say this is the first time I've seen this. "Hello Semantha." She kind of holds on to me, then crawls off and continues to be curious about the room. It's wonderful to see her adapt to taking on new challenges first hesitantly and then forthrightly.

Semantha starts to rub her eyes. I say she seems to be getting tired, and it is time to go, so they pack up their things. Before they leave, I give Caz a card and say, "Open it the day of the party, or the following Monday, which is Semantha's birthday."

The card reads:

Dear Caz,

Please wish Semantha a very Happy First Birthday for me. But, this is also your day—a special Mother's Day. It's been rewarding and my pleasure to get to know you and see you grow into motherhood and embrace it.

Best wishes to you both.

Warmly,
Dr. Hollman

What Does Caz Learn from Playing with Semantha?

This is a new experience for all of us to be in my office. We all easily adjust to the new setting that feels natural because we all know each other so well. Caz sees how Semantha adapts to a new toy, the puppet, slowly and gradually referencing her mother's expressions and ultimately losing her fear. It's wonderful to see how she copes so well in a new situation and environment. It's rather momentous for Caz and me as well as she comes more into my life, which she seems to enjoy. Our attachment is so positive for all of us as we conclude a whole year together.

You may have in your life with your baby a special relationship with someone else who gets to know you and your baby very well over the course of the year. Treasure that connection as Caz and I did. It's memorable and moving to share in the joy of a baby emerging from birth to one year.

Looking Forward

Research on Secure and Insecure Attachments

Longitudinal Research

In earlier chapters, I mentioned research about observing the face-to-face interactions between babies and their mothers that demonstrated the fascinating topic of *attachment research*. This is the research of the future that will be expanded on as years go by. Since this is an area of future growing research on infancy that you and your baby may even want to be involved in, I want you, as my reader, to be up-to-date.

Researchers were able to look at the quality of a mother and baby's interactions and then predict whether their attachment would be secure or insecure when the baby reached twelve months. These interactions set "the trajectory for patterns of relatedness and intimacy over the lifetime" (Beebe, Cohen, and Lachmannn 2016, 2). Because this is *longitudinal research* it is special and extraordinary. Longitudinal research gives us predictions of how the past affects the baby's future.

It is my pleasure to share this with you, because I had the wonderful opportunity to observe these interactive videos firsthand in the studio of Dr. Beatrice Beebe with other infant observers like myself. I want to highlight the findings so you, too, can feel the importance and direct personal relevance of this work for you and your baby's relationship now and in the future.

If you recall, the researchers observed four-month-old babies that were facing and playing naturally with their mothers via video. The video screen was split so that a frontal view of each mother and baby could be observed closely second by second. It is outstanding what a mother and baby can communicate through simple and quick facial, vocal, and gestural expressions—some moments of interaction lasting only one third of a second (5)!

The study of these interactions and future outcomes for babies and parents led to the development of attachment theory. In short, researchers found early interactions impacted future behaviors such as the nature of the reunion of twelve-month-old babies separated briefly from their mothers. As this research is so important to infant development and play, let's look at types of secure versus insecure attachments between parent and child and how these concepts were derived.

Strange Situation Paradigm

The differences between insecure and secure attachments can best be described with the "strange situation paradigm" (Ainsworth et al. 1978). This paradigm simply examines how infants and mothers reunite after a brief separation. During the experiment, the baby plays with her mother in a room. Then a researcher comes in to be with the baby, and the mother leaves the room. When the mother returns, the baby's reaction is observed to determine what the baby's attachment to the mother is like. In other words, how a baby responds to play, separation, and reunion with the mother is evaluated.

The *strange situation* observations are conducted between twelve and eighteen months. It yields four categories of attachment: *avoidant* (A), *secure* (B), *resistant* (C), and *disorganized* (D).

In the *secure* (B) pattern, you as the mother are sensitive to your infant's needs; in turn, your infant tends to use you as a secure base. Your baby will react positively after your reunion by actively engaging with you and recovering easily from the separation.

Recall my sessions with Caz and Semantha where Caz did a great mothering job at creating a secure attachment to her baby over many months' time even when she had to leave for a few days and even when she had to hospitalize her baby, a difficult, scary time that worked out well. Because Semantha's attachment to Caz was so secure, even this hospital experience was not traumatic for either mother or baby.

The other attachment patterns contain differing degrees of insecure attachments. In the *insecure/avoidant pattern* (A), mothers are insensitive to their infants' needs and may be under-involved or intrusive (Belsky, Rovine, and Taylor 1984). Infants of these mothers avoided closeness upon reunion. Thus, these babies need more help in gaining a secure feeling with their mother as their home base.

In the *insecure/resistant pattern* (C), mothers are inconsistent in their responses—sometimes the mothers are non-nurturant, often showing direct interference in the baby's activities, but at other times they are sensitive and caring. The result of this inconsistency is that the infants don't explore their environments much, but instead strongly seek to maintain close proximity with their mothers showing repeated expressions of anger, crying, and petulance. Because these infants are unable to be separated from their mothers, they remain unhappy and do not play during the separation or resume play after the separation when reunited with their mothers.

Again, remembering Caz and Semantha, Caz worried that Semantha didn't sufficiently miss her when she was at day care. Yet, the baby's smiling response at the reunion with Caz illustrated well that their attachment was indeed not insecure, but secure. Caz also discovered that when she went out of the room, Semantha stopped playing because she was focused on her mother's absence and stared at the door. Thus, secure Semantha had found her own way of coping with the separation without distress, resuming her play when her mother came back into the room.

Infants who did not fit into the above patterns resulted in an additional classification: *disorganized/disoriented* (D) infants. These babies show interrupted movements and expressions, display both approach and avoidance patterns, and are confused and apprehensive sometimes resulting in feeling immobilized momentarily. They seem inconsolable in spite of efforts by their mothers to comfort them, and they are unable to separate from their mother and resume play after separation (Beebe et al. 2010, 19).

If this is the case, the attachment can be repaired with gentle intervention with a professional who can support the mother in gaining the trust of her baby turning a disorganized/insecure attachment into a secure one for the future.

In sum, the researchers discovered that by four to six months patterns of mother-infant interaction and communication could be observed and predictable. These patterns predicted how mothers and their babies were attached by twelve to eighteen months at which time secure babies played happily with their mothers after being reunited with them after separation, while other babies became insecure, avoidant, and distressed unable to explore their environments, interact well, and play.

Regarding Play

So, if Beebe et al. (2010) were able to predict a mother and baby's later attachment from when the baby was only four months old, what does this teach us about our early interactions—our *play* with our babies?

The most significant and unlikely distressing classification (D) is disorganized attachment. Researchers found that infants with this attachment would later struggle to deal with negative emotions because the mother denies the baby's distress with a controlling style that is not empathic (109). She does not understand her baby's reactions and thus cannot offer a nurturing response. Instead she may take over the baby's activity which only upsets the baby because they are not in synch.

However, mothers can learn to empathize with their babies even if they have never had that maternal influence themselves. This is the wonder of infant-parent psychotherapy that I have engaged in. I've had the opportunity to witness mothers who initially didn't intuitively understand their babies' communications and emotions become able to learn over a reasonable period of time how to connect emotionally with their infants, giving both mothers and babies more joy.

Throughout the earlier chapters, we have discussed the importance of being attuned to your baby and his emotions and showing empathy and care during your play. The disorganized infants in the above study are a perfect example of why these things are important. The play their mothers had with them at the four-month juncture was severely compromised in timing, quality of interaction, and empathy. Perhaps these infants are thinking:

> I don't know what you feel. You show me incomprehensible, indigestible smiling and surprised faces when I am upset; your face is inscrutable. I can't count on your attention. I don't know when you are going to loom into my face. I can't read your intent, and I feel threatened. I can't influence you to follow my facial-visual changes or my touch. I can't read you or predict you; you are not on my wavelength. (110)

This disconnect between mother and baby can change with effective intervention with the pair by a well-trained infant-parent psychotherapist. After reading the play suggestions month by month, you now have the tools to address infant distress in a playful, loving way. If you find this difficult, then of course it's wise and satisfying to seek guidance from a professional.

As you now see, the importance of learning how to play with your infant can have significant results—early play from the start has its effects throughout the baby's twelve months that are confirmed by their level of attachment at one year!

Mothers who have extreme difficulty having positive interactions should not be blamed, however, as they have long histories of long-term distress of their own. If this is of concern to you, due to difficulties you may have experienced in your life, you can feel heartened to know this can effectively become a new learning process for you as a mother, one you can undertake successfully over time with guidance. You can gain, in your generation with your baby, an entirely new positive way of interacting and giving and receiving love.

While this research is sometimes daunting, it is essential and important to realize that mismatched states between mother and infant are common but quickly repairable. It's just part of everyday life with your baby.

Actually, research has shown this over and over (Beebe, Cohen, and Lachmannn 2016). In other words, you don't have to be perfect! Secure attachments are easily built through intentional play that takes into consideration the interactions of the mother's and baby's minds. Inevitably, there will be a mishap here and there that you will pick up and attend to effectively to sustain your baby's secure attachment with you. In fact, simply playing repeatedly with your infant intentionally and empathically will only strengthen your relationship with your baby. Your babies will learn to trust you will provide safety and security as they become mobile and continually fascinated by the world around them.

―❧―

Learning how to play with your infant and monitoring your affective or emotional interactions can be a positive and enjoyable experience for both you and your infant. You are now equipped with examples and ideas that will hopefully help you to create positive attuned experiences with your baby—now and in the future.

As you focus on your little one's needs, emotions, preferences, and emerging personality, you will promote a lasting,
secure attachment that will aid your baby in learning how to regulate his own emotions and live a life full of positive interactions
and loving relationships.

References

Books and Journal Articles

Ainsworth, Mary D. Salter. 1967. *Infancy in Uganda: Infant Care and the Growth of Love*. Baltimore: Johns Hopkins University Press.

Ainsworth, Mary D. Salter, Mary C. Blehar, Everett Waters, and Sally N. Wall. 1978. *Patterns of Attachment: A Psychological Study of the Strange Situation*. Hillsdale, NJ: Erlbaum.

Ammaniti, Massimo, and Cristina Trentini. 2009. "How New Knowledge about Parenting Reveals the Neurobiological Implications of Intersubjectivity: A Conceptual Synthesis of Recent Research." *Psychoanalytic Dialogues* 19(5): 537–555.

Bates, Elizabeth. 1979. "Intentions, Conventions and Symbols." In E. Bates (Ed.), *The Emergence of Symbols: Cognition and Communication in Infancy*. New York: Academic Press.

Beebe, Beatrice. 2000. "Co-constructing Mother-Infant Distress." *Psychoanalytic Inquiry* 20: 421–440.

Beebe, Beatrice. 2014. "My Journey in Infant Research and Psychoanalysis: Microanalysis, A Social Microscope." *Psychoanalytic Psychology* 31(1): 4–25.

Beebe, Beatrice, Phyllis Cohen, and Frank Lachmann. 2016. *The Mother-Infant Interaction Picture Book: Origins of Attachment*. New York: Norton & Co., Inc.

Beebe, Beatrice, Joseph Jaffe, Sara Markese, Karen Buck, Henian Chen, Patricia Cohen, Lorraine Bahrick, Howard Andrews, and Stanley Feldstein. 2010. "The Origins of 12-Month Attachment: A Microanalysis of 4-Month Mother-Infant Interaction." *Attachment and Human Development* 12: (1–2), 6–188.

Belsky, Jay, Michael Rovine, Dawn G. Taylor. 1984. "The Pennsylvania Infant and Family Development Project, III: The Origins of Individual Differences in Infant-Mother Attachment: Maternal and Infant Contributions." *Child Development* 55: 718–728.

Brazelton, T. Berry. 1969. *Infants and Mothers: Differences in Development*. University of Michigan: Delacorte.

Brazelton, T. Berry. 1992. "Touch and the Fetus." Presented to Touch Research Institute, Miami, FL (May).

Brazelton, T. Berry. 2006. *Touchpoints: Birth to Three*. Cambridge, MA: Da Capo Press.

Carpendale, Jenny, and Charlie Lewis. 2008. *How Children Develop Social Understanding*. Malden, MA: Blackwell.

Freud, Anna. 1965. *Normality and Pathology in Childhood: Assessments of Development*. New York: International Universities Press.

Gergely, György, and John S. Watson. 1996. "The Social
Biofeedback Theory of Parental-Affect-Mirroring: The
Development of Emotional Self-Awareness and Self-Control in
Infancy." *The International Journal of Psycho-Analysis* 77:1–31.

Gopnik, Alison, Andrew N. Meltzoff, and Patricia K. Kuhl. 1999.
The Scientist in the Crib: What Early Learning Tells Us about the Mind.
New York: HarperCollins.

Greenspan, Stanley L. 1997. *Infancy and Early Childhood.* Madison,
CT: International Universities Press, Inc.

Haith, Marshall M., Cindy Hazen, and Gail S. Goodman. 1988.
"Expectation and Anticipation of Dynamic Visual Events by
3.5-Month-Old Babies." *Child Development* 59(2): 467–79.

Insel, Thomas R., and Larry J. Young. 2001. "The Neurobiology
of Attachment." *Nature Review Neuroscience* 2: 129–136.

Izard, Carroll E. 1978. "On the Ontogenesis of Emotions and the
Emotion-Cognition Relationship in Infancy." In M. Lewis and L.A.
Rosenblum (Eds.), *The Development of Affect.* New York: Plenum Press.

Kernberg, Paulina. 2006. *Beyond the Reflection: The Role of the Mirror
Paradigm in Clinical Practice.* New York: Other Press LLC.

Lamb, Michael E., and Lonnie R. Sherrod, eds. 1981. *Infant
Social Cognition: Empirical and Theoretical Considerations.* Oxford:
Psychology Press.

Mahler, Margaret, Fred Pine, and Anni Bergman. 1975. *The
Psychological Birth of the Human Infant.* New York: Basic Books.

Mahon, E. 1993. "Play, Parenthood and Creativity." In A. Solnit,
D. Cohen, and P. Neubauer (Eds.), *The Many Meanings of Play: A
Psychoanalytic Perspective.* New Haven, CT: Yale University Press.

McDevitt, John B. 1979. "The Role of Internalization in the Development of Object Relations during the Separation-Individuation Phase." *Journal of the American Psychoanalytic Association* 27: 327–43.

Meltzoff, Andrew N. 1990. "Foundations for Developing a Concept of Self: The Role of Imitation in Relating Self to Other and the Value of Social Mirroring, Social Modeling, and Self-Practice in Infancy." In D. Cicchetti and M. Beeghly Marjorie (Eds.), *The Self in Transition: Infancy to Childhood.* Norwood, NJ: Ablex.

Meltzoff, Andrew N., and M. Keith Moore. 1983. "Newborn Infants Imitate Adult Facial Gestures." *Child Development* 54 (3): 702–709.

Messer, David J., and Peter M. Vietze. 1984. "Timing and Transitions in Mother-Infant Gaze." *Infant Behavior and Development* 7(2): 167–181.

Murkoff, Heidi, Arlene Eisenberg, and Sandee Hathaway. 2003. *What to Expect the First Year.* New York: Workman.

Nachman, Patricia, and Daniel Stern. 1983. Recall Memory for Emotional Experience in Pre-Linguistic Infants. Paper presented at the National Clinical Infancy Fellows Conference, Yale University, New Haven, CT.

Nitschke, Jack B., Eric Nelson, Brett Rusch, Andrew Fox, Terrence Oakes, and Richard Davidson. 2004. "Orbitofrontal Cortex Tracks Positive Mood in Mothers Viewing Pictures of Their Newborn Infants." *Neuroimage* 21(2): 583–592.

Peery, Craig J. 1980. "Neonate-Adult Head Movement." *Developmental Psychology* 16: 245–250.

Rijt,H., Plooij, F, Plas-Plooj,X. (2019) *The Wonder Weeks*, Norton & Co., New York, New York.

Ritvo, Samuel. 1993. "Play and Illusion." In A. Solnit, D. Cohen, and P. Neubauer (Eds.), *The Many Meanings of Play: A Psychoanalytic Perspective.* New Haven, CT: Yale University Press.

Sieratzki, J.S., and B. Woll. 1996. "Why Do Mothers Cradle Babies on Their Left?" *The Lancet* 347(9017): 1746–1748.

Solnit, Albert J., Donald J. Cohen, and Peter B. Neubauer, eds. 1993. *The Many Meanings of Play: A Psychoanalytic Perspective.* New Haven, CT: Yale University Press.

Spitz, Rene A. 1965. *The First Year of Life.* New York: International Universities Press.

Stern, Daniel N. 1974. "Mother and Infant at Play: The Dyadic Interaction Involving Facial, Vocal and Gaze Behaviors." In Michael Lewis and Leonard A. Rosenblum (Eds.), *The Effect of the Infant on Its Caregiver.* New York: Wiley.

Stern, Daniel N. 1985. *The Interpersonal World of the Infant: A View from Psychoanalysis and Developmental Psychology.* New York: Basic Books.

Stern, Daniel, and Louis Sander. 1980. "New Knowledge about the Infant from Current Research: Implications for Psychoanalysis." *Journal of the American Psychoanalytic Association* 28(1): 181–198.

Trevarthen, Colwyn. 1979. "Communication and Cooperation in Early Infancy: A Description of Primary Intersubjectivity." In Margaret Bullowa (Ed.), *Before Speech: The Beginnings of Human Communication.* London: Cambridge University Press.

Trevarthen, Colwyn, and Kenneth J. Aitken. 2001. "Infant Intersubjectivity: Research, Theory, and Clinical Applications: Annual Research Review." *Journal of Child Psychology and Psychiatry* 42: 3–48.

Van de Rijt, Henry, Frans X. Plooij, and Xaviera Plas-Plooij. 2019. *The Wonder Weeks: A Stress-Free Guide to Your Baby's Behavior*, 6th ed. New York: Countryman Press.

Werner, Heinz. 1948. *The Comparative Psychology of Mental Development*. New York: International Universities Press.

Winnicott, Donald W. 1968. "Playing: Its Theoretical Status in the Clinical Situation." *The International Journal of Psychoanalysis*. 49: 591–599.

Winnicott, Donald W. 1971. *Playing and Reality*. New York: Basic Books.

Websites and Online Articles

Clayton, Jamie. "Playing with Your 8-Month-Old Baby: What to Expect." Bright Hub Education. August 12, 2011. https://www.brighthubeducation.com/infant-development-learning/122977-creative-interaction-for-the-eight-month-old-infant/ (Accessed September 5, 2020).

Easy Baby Life. "11-Month-Old Baby Development Milestones, Activities & Toys!" Open Hands Media AB. https://www.easybabylife.com/11-month-old.html#Games%20to%20play/ (Accessed August 20, 2020).

Halpern, Jennifer. "How Should I Play with a 12-Month-Old?" Parents.com. July 2, 2015. https://www.parents.com/advice/babies/baby-development/how-should-i-play-with-a-12-month-old/ (Accessed September 4).

Henry, Crystal. "Games and Activities for a 7-Month-Old Infant." Hello Motherhood. June 13, 2017. https://www.hellomotherhood.com/article/166123-games-and-activities-for-a-7-month-old-infant/ (Accessed September 4, 2020).

McNamara, Alexander. "Eight-Month-Old Babies Able to Understand Basics of Grammar." Science Focus. March 13, 2020. https://www.sciencefocus.com/news/eight-month-old-babies-able-to-understand-basics-of-grammar/ (Accessed August 24, 2020).

Medical Dictionary. *The Free Dictionary*. s.v. "Proprioception." https://medical-dictionary.thefreedictionary.com/proprioception (Accessed September 2, 2020).

New Kids Center. "Activities for Your 11 Months Old Baby." NewKidsCenter.com. https://www.newkidscenter.com/Activities-For-11-Month-Old.html/ (Accessed September 4, 2020).

Open Hands Media AB. "The 5-Month-Old Baby – Development Milestones, Fun Activities, Toy Tips." Easy Baby Life. https://www.easybabylife.com/5-month-old.html/ (Accessed August 29, 2020).

Semerda, Urszula. "Month 10: Top 10 Sensory Activities for Your 10 Month Old Baby." Sensory Lifestyle. https://www.sensorylifestyle.com/activities-0-24-months/month-10-top-10-sensory-activities-for-your-10-month-old/ (Accessed August 27, 2020).

wikiHow. "How to Play with 12-Month-Old Baby." Wikihow.
com. Updated November 3, 2018. https://www.wikihow.com/
Play-with-a-12-Month-Old-Baby (Accessed September 4, 2020).

Additional Resources

Books and Journal Articles

Bates, E. 1979. "Intentions, Conventions and Symbols." In E. Bates (Ed.), *The Emergence of Symbols: Cognition and Communication in Infancy*. New York: Academic Press.

Gergely, G., and J.S. Watson. 1999. "Early Socio-emotional Development: Contingency Perception and the Social-Biofeedback Model." In P. Rochat (Ed.), *Early Social Cognition: Understanding Others in the First Months of Life*. Hillsdale, NJ: Erlbaum, 101–137.

Hofer, S. 1990. "Early Symbiotic Processes: Hard Evidence from a Soft Place." In S. Bone and R. Glick (Eds.), *Pleasure beyond the Pleasure Principle*. New Haven: Yale University Press.

Horton, P.C. 1995. "The Comforting Substrate and the Right Brain." *Bulletin of the Menninger Clinic* 59(4): 480–486.

Jaffee, Joseph, Beatrice Beebe, Stanley Feldstein, Cynthia L. Crown, Michael D. Jasnow, Philippe Rochat, and Daniel N. Stern. 2001. *Rhythms of Dialogue in Infancy: Coordinated Timing and*

Development (Monograph of the Society for Research in Child Development). Malden, MA: Blackwell.

Lenzi, Delia, Cristina Trentini, Emiliano Macaluso, Massimo Ammaniti, Gianluigi Lenzi, and Patrizia Pantano. 2006. "Neurobiological Basis of Maternal Empathy: Evidence from fMRI." *NeuroImage* 31(Suppl.): S89.

Lenzi, D., C. Trentini, P. Patano, E. Macaluso, M. Iacoboni, G.L. Lenzi, and M. Ammantiti. 2008. "Neural Basis of Maternal Communication and Emotional Expressions Processing during the Infant Preverbal Stage." *Cerebral Cortex* 19(5): 1124–1133.

Manning, J.T., R.L. Trivers, R. Thorhill, D. Singh, J. Denman, M.H. Eklo, and R.H. Anderton. 1997. "Ear Asymmetry and Left-Side Cradling." *Evolution and Human Behavior* 18(5): 327–340.

Papousek, D. 1979. "Early Ontogeny of Human Social Interaction: Its Biological Roots and Social Dimensions." In M. von Cranach, K. Foppa, W. Lepenies, and D. Ploog (Eds.), *Human Ethology: Claims and Limits of a New Discipline.* New York: Cambridge University Press. 456–478.

Schaffer, H.R. 1977. *Studies in Infancy.* London: Academic Press.

Schore, A.N. 1994. *Affect Regulation and the Origin of the Self: The Neurobiology of Emotional Development.* Mahwah, NJ: Erlbaum.

Schore, A.N. 2003. *Affect Dysregulation and Disorder of the Self.* New York: Norton.

Sostek, C. 1980. "Neonate-Adult Head Viewing Pictures of Their Newborn Infants." *Neuroimage* 21: 583–592.

Stern, D.N. 1974. "The Goal and Structure of Mother-Infant Play." *Journal of the American Academy of Child and Adolescent Psychiatry* 13, 402–421.

Trevarthen, C. 2005. "First Things First: Infants Make Good Use of the Sympathetic Rhythm of Imitation, without Reason or Language." *Journal of Child Psychotherapy* 31: 191–113.

Trevarthen, C., and P. Hubley. 1978. "Secondary Intersubjectivity: Confidence, Confiders and Acts of Meaning in the First Year." In A. Lock (Ed.), *Action, Gesture and Symbol: The Emergence of Language.* New York: Academic Press.

Watson, J.S. 1979. Perception of Contingency as a Determinant of Social Responsiveness. In E. Thomas (Ed.), *The Origins of Social Responsiveness.* Hillsdale, NJ: Erlbaum.

Watson, J.S. 1980. "Bases of Causal Inference in Infancy: Time, Space, and Sensory Relations. Paper presented at the International Conference on Infant Studies. New Haven, CT.

Websites and Online Articles

Baby Centre UK. "Toddler Mini Spa." BabyCentre LLC. https://www.babycentre.co.uk/a1045895/toddler-mini-spa/ (Accessed August 28, 2020).

Grayson, Lee. "Activities for a 2-Month-Old." Hello Motherhood. November 28, 2018. https://www.hellomotherhood.com/article/113199-activities-2monthold-infant/ (Accessed August 28, 2020).

Great Dad. "How to Play with Your Ten-Month-Old Baby." GreatDad.com. https://www.greatdad.com/baby/how-to-play-with-your-ten-month-old-baby/ (Accessed August 22, 2020).

Halpern, Jennifer. "How Should I Play with a Seven-Month-Old?" Parents.com. July 2, 2015. https://www.parents.com/advice/babies/baby-development/how-should-i-play-with-a-7-month-old/ (Accessed September 4, 2020).

Halpern, Jennifer. "How Should I Play with a Nine-Month-Old?" Parents.com. July 2, 2015. https://www.parents.com/advice/babies/baby-development/how-should-i-play-with-a-9-month-old/ (Accessed September 4, 2020).

Halpern, Jennifer. "How Should I Play with a Ten-Month-Old?" Parents.com. July 2, 2015.https://www.parents.com/advice/babies/baby-development/how-should-i-play-with-a-10-month-old/ (Accessed September 4, 2020).

Healthy Children. "Transitional Objects." American Academy of Pediatrics. Updated August 1, 2009. https://www.healthychildren.org/English/ages-stages/baby/Pages/Transitional-Objects.aspx/ (Accessed August 9, 2020).

Loop, Erika. "How to Entertain a 1-Year-Old." How to Adult. April 18, 2017. https://howtoadult.com/play-with-10-6471.html/ (Accessed August 15, 2020).

Slaton, Joyce. "20 Fun, Silly, Development-Boosting Games to Play with Your Baby." Baby Center. https://www.babycenter.com/0_20-fun-silly-development-boosting-games-to-play-with-your-ba_1479310.bc/ (Accessed August 7, 2020).

Web MD. "Baby Development Milestones." Grow by Web MD. https://www.webmd.com/parenting/baby/baby-development-milestones-directory (Accessed August 14, 2019).

Web MD. "Baby Development: Your 2-Month Old." Grow by Web MD. Reviewed March 23, 2019. https://www.webmd.com/parenting/baby/baby-development-2-month-old#1 (Accessed September 2, 2020).

What to Expect. "5-Month-Old." WhatToExpect.com. Reviewed December 26, 2018. https://www.whattoexpect.com/first-year/month-by-month/month-5.aspx (Accessed August 12, 2020).

What to Expect. "Recognizing Objects, People and Self." WhatToExpect.com. Reviewed October 7, 2016. https://www.whattoexpect.com/toddler/self-recognition/ (Accessed August 20, 2020).

Index

B

E

eighth month, babies 145–160; **infant development** 147–
150; **object permanence** 145–160; **parents and** 155–160;
playtime suggestions 150–154; **researchers** 145–146

Eisenberg, Arlene 98, 133, 147, 173

eleventh month, babies 197–205; **imagining stories** 197–
205; infant development 198; **mother and** 200–205; **play**
suggestions 199–200; **researchers** 197–198

embodied simulation 84

emotional attunement see tenth month, babies

emotions/emotional 29–32, 81; **attunement** 183–
195; **development** 46–47, 211; **exchanges** 167;
experience 114–116; **expressions** 9; **gesturing** 16–17;
security 16; **states** 166; **warmth** 13

engrossed fathers 8

existential questions 167

experiment concerning attunement 185

exploring categories 170–171

external behavior 22

eye-to-eye orientations 31, 34

F

face-to-face interaction 78–80, 87, 102, 223

facial expressions 9, 16–17, 22, 24, 34, 46–47, 80–82, 112,
120, 123, 132, 184, 191; see also subtle facial expressions

facial recognition 33–34

fathers: as engrossed 8; **tenth month, babies and** 191–195

feelings 14

feeling state 183–184

G

H

R

S

About the Author

L aurie Hollman, PhD, is a psychoanalyst with specialized clinical training in infant-parent, child, adolescent, and adult psychotherapy and is an expert on the Narcissistic Personality Disorder.

She is an authority on modern parent-child relationships and is an award-winning author who has published seven books. She has been on the faculties of New York University and the Society for Psychoanalytic Training and Research, among others.

She has written extensively on parenting for various publications, including *The Psychoanalytic Study of the Child, The International Journal of Infant Observation and Its Applications, The Inner World of the Mother, Newsday's Parents & Children Magazine*, and *Long Island Parent in New York*. She blogged for *Huffington Post* and currently contributes articles for *Thrive Global, MindBodyGreen, UpJourney*, and *Authority Magazine*. She also writes for *Active Family Magazine* in San Francisco and is a parenting expert for *Good Housekeeping* and *Bustle Lifestyle*.

Her Gold Mom's Choice Award–winning books are *Unlocking Parental Intelligence: Finding Meaning in Your Child's Behavior* with companion award-winning books *The Busy Parent's Guide to Managing Anxiety in Children and Teens: The Parental Intelligence Way* and *The*

Busy Parent's Guide to Managing Anger in Children and Teens: The Parental Intelligence Way.

Other books in this series are *The Busy Parent's Guide to Managing Technology with Children and Teens: The Parental Intelligence Way* and *The Busy Parent's Guide to Managing Exhaustion with Children and Teens: The Parental Intelligence Way.*

She has also written *Are You Living with a Narcissist? How Narcissistic Men Impact Your Happiness, How to Identify Them, and How to Avoid Raising One.*

She is proud to be an adoring and loving wife, mother, and grandmother.